Rebound 1993

Workshop Models for Family Life Education

STRESS MANAGEMENT

Kathryn Apgar
and
Betsy Nicholson Callahan

Family Service Association of America
44 East 23rd Street
New York, New York 10010

Library of Congress Cataloging in Publication Data

Apgar, Kathryn.
    Stress management.

    (Workshop models for family life education)
    1. Stress (Psychology)--Prevention--Study and teaching
I. Callahan, Betsy Nicholson. II. Title. III. Series.
BF575.S75A63   158'.1   82-5096
ISBN 0-87304-189-5

Printed in the U.S.A.

TABLE OF CONTENTS

FOREWORD

Are we better off today in terms of life-style than were our parents
and grandparents? Initially, our reaction would have to be that we
surely are, that indeed these are the "best of times"! As we consider the many improvements in the quality of life, the conveniences
that have been developed for home and work, improved communication,
improvements in sanitation, the diminished number of infectious diseases, who could disagree? Think of all those who have become
increasingly enfranchised by law, vote, or education. Could anyone
argue that as a nation we are not materially and physically better off
than previous generations?

Unfortunately, these legal and technological gains are not the whole
story. When we take a second look at the world around us, we see
that new problems have arisen in place of old. If we scratch the
surface of our seeming satisfaction, we can detect a new form of
epidemic, although it is a more silent one. This new epidemic is
made up of the stress-induced diseases of human beings. In place of
the old worries, society has nurtured a whole new set of problems.

What are those forces in society that have given birth to these
stress-induced diseases? For many of us, economic survival is no
less of a problem than it was for previous generations. Inflation,
recession, and unemployment are front-page headlines every day.
Nuclear conflict and nuclear holocaust are never more than a push
button away. In place of infectious diseases, we now worry about
heart disease, hypertension, and other stress-related diseases. In
our society, there are relatively few of us who have to worry about
malnutrition. But is there a family who does not have at least one

person who worries about weight control and is there anyone who does not worry from time to time about the toxins and carcinogens in their meals?

What about our personal and family relationships? The increased mobility of the nuclear family, the loss of support from the breakup of the extended family, the changing role of women at home and on the job have all affected our lives in dramatic ways. How do we as parents cope with our children under such circumstances?

What has happened to the institutions that we used to depend on? Church and synagogue, government, schools, the medical structure are all in a state of transition. Old values are being challenged on a daily basis. Are we indeed "better-off" than were our parents and grandparents?

From this point of view, it would seem that society is as threatened today as our ancestors were by plague or famine. Because the problems are subtle, there is a surface calm to our daily lives. This calm, however, is based more upon denial and a false bravado than a genuine confrontation with the realities. Surely, we are all potential victims!

How can we protect ourselves from the new affliction? Is there a model from the past that we can borrow? We protected ourselves in the past by a program of primary prevention; we do the same for this new crop of stress-induced diseases. We may not have vaccines against stress as we do against polio and smallpox but we _are_ developing a vast armamentaria of dealing with stress. We can find ways

of preventing stress from afflicting us in such a way as to bring
about maladaptive behavior.

The Family Service Association of Greater Boston has developed this
stress management workshop model as an excellent method of preventing
stress. What are some of its unique features? Stress and its emotional and physical effects are the universal complaint of man. All
people experience stress regardless of their status in life. While
we cannot avoid it, we _can_ find ways of dealing with it more adaptively. This workshop looks at how stress invades our daily lives in
ways that we may have overlooked. We are given the opportunity to
discover how we, as individuals, cope with stress both positively
and negatively.

Furthermore, the workshop provides us with interesting information
about the nature of stress, how the mind and body interact, and how
we may make our bodies "victims" of stress. The objective is to
help us work out why we become ill with certain kinds of diseases and
health problems.

We are not empty-handed in dealing with stress. We all have many
skills and strengths at our disposal. The workshop suggests ways
that we can take charge and reorganize our lives to make them no
less challenging but _not_ overwhelming. We are even asked to take a
second look at time and how we might make it our servant rather than
be enslaved by it.

A number of ways are provided to help people regain mastery of their
selves and become reacquainted with their bodies. People learn to

identify how stress affects various parts of the body. A variety of relaxation exercises and techniques is incorporated into the program.

The stress management workshop is but one of the many family life education programs that have been developed. These programs share a number of objectives in common: The participants learn skills in communication, relationship building, problem solving, decision making, and life planning. Participants set objectives, make choices, share various points of view, provide feedback to one another, and learn how to listen. No one family life education program can provide all the answers. There are many problems in life that need special consideration. Other family life education programs include topics covering planning for a career, coping with divorce, the problems of widowhood. Nevertheless, mastering the skills outlined in this stress management workshop is a natural bridge to ultimately dealing with any of the unique and special stresses that life will inevitably bring to each and every one of us.

It is impossible to eliminate stress from life. It is not only woven into the fabric of life, it is at the root of our creativity and progress. Our task is to learn how to deal with it adaptively. The program outlined in this manual provides an excellent way of doing so.

Howard S. King, M.D.
Newton Lower Falls, Massachusetts

PREFACE

Workshop Models for Family Life Education is a series of manuals intended to promote the exploration of new alternatives and the utilization of new options in day-to-day living through programs in family life education.

Basically, family life education (FLE) is a service of planned intervention that applies the dynamic process of group learning to improving the quality of individual and family living. The manuals are in workshop format and offer possible new approaches of service to families. They are meant to serve as a training mechanism and basic framework for group leaders involved in FLE workshops.

In 1974, the Family Service Association of America (FSAA) appointed a National Task Force on Family Life Education, Development, and Enrichment. One of the goals of the task force was to assess the importance and future direction of family life education services within family service agencies. One of the recommendations of its report was to "recognize family life education, development, and enrichment as one of the three major services of the family service agency: family counseling, family life education, and family advocacy."[1] This recommendation was adopted by the Board of Directors of FSAA and has become basic policy of the association.

---

1. "Overview of Findings of the FSAA Task Force on Family Life Education, Development, and Enrichment," mimeographed (New York: Family Service Association of America, May 1976), p. 21.

An interest in family life education is a natural development of FSAA's role in the strengthening of family life and complementary to the more traditional remedial functions of family agencies. FLE programs can add a new dimension to the services provided by family agencies. They can open an agency to the general population by providing programs which are appropriate for all families and individuals, not only for those at risk. They provide a new arena for service that deals with growth as well as dysfunction. They can encourage agencies to look beyond the therapeutic approach and to take on a new objective for the enrichment and strengthening of family life. For the participants, FLE programs can lead to increased understanding of normal stress, growth of esteem for one's self and others, development of communications skills, improved ability to cope with problem situations, development of problem-solving skills, and maximization of family and individual potential.

This series provides tangible evidence of FSAA's continuing interest in family life education and of a belief in its future importance for family services. FLE programs, coordinated within a total agency program and viewed as a vital and integral part of the agency, can become key factors in family service concern for growth and development within all families.

GENERAL INFORMATION
ABOUT THE WORKSHOP

PROMOTING THE GROUP

WORK WITH A COSPONSOR. Cosponsoring the program with another well-
known and respected organization in the community that works with
adults can greatly help in the recruitment of group members. We
have found a strong interest in stress management among working
people. Business, industry, unions, schools, community colleges,
professional groups, hospital employees might want to cosponsor a
group. Determine who the key decision-making person is and make an
appointment to discuss your program; ideally, arrange to have someone from the organization who knows the person introduce you. We
have presented stress management training workshops for employees
of the New England Telephone Company, the Boston Housing Authority,
Computervision, Quincy City Hospital, and federal employees, as well
as for a statewide teacher's union--the Massachusetts Teachers
Association, and classes at Quincy Women's Center and the Weymouth
Adult Education program.

FLYERS. Having a brief, attractive, eye-catching flyer is an effective way to promote the workshop. If you work in a human services
organization, send a flyer to all members of the staff with a brief
cover memo, and ask them to review their client lists and let you
know of people they think would benefit from the group. Also, contact any organizations or facilities in the area that come into
contact with the population you hope to attract, and send flyers to
them for distribution.

1

USE OF PUBLICITY. Make use of your community's free publicity sources. Radio stations, newspapers, and television stations offer free public service announcements. A brief description of the workshop (dates, place, and so on) and dates to air the announcement should be sent to the public service director of the media chosen. Contact local stations and newspapers for the format each requires for such announcements and for deadline dates. Note, too, that some newspapers may be willing to print a short article on the workshop. This provides greater visibility than a public service announcement. It is usually necessary to write a formal news release for this.

Many organizations have house organs or newsletters that are distributed periodically to all employees. Contact the person responsible for inserting announcements and give a brief description of the workshop. Some organizations may be interested in coupling the announcement of the workshop with a feature article about stress on the job in their business.

TIPS FOR ENSURING GOOD ATTENDANCE

It is a good idea to speak with every applicant on the telephone before the workshop begins. This allows participants to establish an official contact with the group leader ahead of time, to ask questions, and to iron out any difficulties that might prevent them from attending the workshop.

Often, one or two people are unable to attend the first session. They may or may not call to tell you; if you do not call or write them, they may be lost to the group. Usually a letter stating that you are sorry they missed the first session and offering a fifteen minute pregroup make-up session is successful. This enables you to talk to them personally and discuss whether they really want to join the group. Introducing new members and having them share their goals at Session 2 will help integrate them into the group. Planning for, and expecting to add, new members at Session 2 also gives you leeway to add latecomers. You can add up to six new people if you use a pregroup orientation session and spend part of the regular session introducing old and new members. It is not good for group cohesion to add anyone after the second meeting.

At the first session, explain that the workshop is most successful when participants attend every meeting. Ask them to please call you prior to the meeting time if they are unable to attend. If they miss a session and do not call, contact them. Avoid making members feel guilty about missing a session and be very supportive so that they will feel welcome to return. It is important to them that you care enough to miss their presence and to keep them up-to-date; if they feel they have missed too much, it becomes very easy to drop out. If you send handouts and a brief note to those who miss a session, they will generally attend the next session.

Persistent follow-up and personal contact are your keys to success.

LEADER'S PREPARATION

Most important, read the workshop guide very carefully and plan how to handle each portion of the workshop. You should be familiar enough with the contents so you will not have to consult the manual at every moment. This manual is for you; the instructions are written for your use and the material presented within quotation marks is for you to use in talking with the group. The more spontaneous your presentation is, and the more responsive you are to the participants, the more effective the workshop will be.

LENGTH. There are seven sessions in this model, which is planned to cover a seven-week period. Each session requires two hours.

MATERIALS. All of the materials used in the workshop are relatively inexpensive and readily available. Most sessions require:

    flipchart or chalkboard
    felt markers or chalk
    note pads
    pens or pencils
    5" x 8" unlined cards for name tags
    safety pins or masking tape
    copies of the handouts for each session

MINI-LECTURES. The manual provides basic information for each mini-lecture. Present mini-lectures in your own words, modifying them to suit your style and your group. You will be most effective if you adapt the mini-lecture to fit the group's learning needs, expectations, and past learning experiences. You may decide to spend more time on one section than another, adding your own material or modifications. Be creative!

For example, as noted in the manual, some mini-lectures may be most effective when presented directly by you, while others may serve mainly as background, with open discussion being the primary means of covering the material.

You may want to practice presenting some of the material ahead of time. A simple and informal way to present mini-lecture material is to list key ideas on a flipchart or chalkboard ahead of time. This list serves as a guide for your talk. Also, groups tend to respond more positively when mini-lectures include such visual aids.

We recommend that you limit lectures to fifteen minutes to allow time for exercises and discussion. From our experience, participants learn more from active involvement than from simply listening to presentations.

BRIEF OUTLINES. A brief outline is provided for each session. You can display this on a flipchart or chalkboard and go over it at the start of the workshop. This lets the group know what is to be covered that day. You should fill in the time for each section of the workshop after deciding what you will be covering and estimating how long each activity should run.

HOME ASSIGNMENTS. All sessions require some outside activity such as practice of the relaxation techniques. Go over the assignment and emphasize that you will discuss it at the next session--then be sure to do it. A good time to begin the discussion is as people are arriving. Encourage the group to complete the assignment, but do not pressure participants to do so.

HANDOUTS. Each session has a section of sample handout materials. A workbook, with all of the handout materials necessary for participants, is available for this workshop model. Handouts should be sent to absentees with a brief note to let them know they were missed by the group.

LEADER'S ROLE

You will be filling many roles--facilitator, resource person, teacher. A knowledge of group processes, adult learning theory, and human growth and development will contribute to your success in conducting workshops. Beginning leaders may wish to adhere closely to the original model, while more experienced leaders may decide to use sections of the material selectively. We encourage you to be creative and flexible in using the models, and to adapt them to your own style.

SESSION 1

BRIEF OUTLINE

OBJECTIVES: To involve the participants in the workshop through introductions, and in the process of objective setting.

To define stress; to teach participants deep muscle relaxation and to allow them opportunity to practice this stress management technique.

I. INTRODUCTION--GETTING ACQUAINTED

    A. Fill Out Name Tags
    B. Leader Introduces Self
    C. Purpose of Workshop

II. SETTING OBJECTIVES

III. STRESS SIMULATION

IV. MINI-LECTURE: WHAT IS STRESS

V. DEEP MUSCLE RELAXATION

    A. Mini-lecture
    B. Exercise

VI. HOME ASSIGNMENT

    HANDOUTS

SESSION 1

I. INTRODUCTION--GET ACQUAINTED

A. Fill Out Name Tags

Before the workshop, prepare 5" x 8" index cards for name tags; see the sample on page 9. Have felt markers and safety pins available.

Put the instructions for completing the name tag on a flipchart or chalkboard.

As people arrive ask them to put their names in the center and then to fill out the rest of the name tag according to the instructions on the flipchart or chalkboard.

Sample Name Tag

Please place your answers to the following questions in the appropriate corner:

1. What is your definition of stress?

2. How do you cope with stress?

3. What are your goals for the workshop?

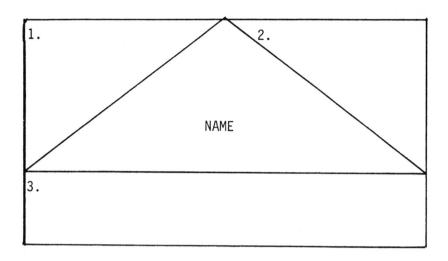

1.

2.

NAME

3.

B. Leader Introduces Self

Give your name, position, title, and perhaps your formal and special training and background relevant to stress management. Describe how you will be handling the role of leader: structuring and acting as facilitator and resource person.

C. Purpose of Workshop

"This workshop is designed to help you learn and practice skills to cope more effectively with the stress we all experience as a result of living in today's fast-paced world.[1] In this technologically advanced society we are all affected

---

1. This material and sections of the balance of the manual are based on material by the authors that appeared in "Stress Management," in Workshop Models for Family Life Education: Four One-Day Workshops, published by Resource Communications, Inc., Boston, Massachusetts, in cooperation with the Family Service Association of America. The material has been reprinted with permission of the publisher.

by stress, no matter what our age--young or old. Every day
each of us has to adapt to unexpected change--a major source
of stress in itself. In our relationships between the sexes,
the guidelines men and women once followed are no longer held
valid. Uncertainty and change are the norm. Just to survive
requires mental vigilance and constant adaptation. The price
we pay is in stress and stress-related disease,

"Each of you could give examples from your experience of
stress in your life; however, an unburdening of personal 'war
stories' has a useful but short-lived effect. The goals for
this workshop are designed to surpass this cathartic effect.
Most of you probably know something about stress, especially
some of the harmful effects such as high blood pressure, tension headaches, ulcers, and insomnia. But few people really
understand fully what stress is, and how to prevent or
alleviate some of its harmful effects.

"The three major goals for the workshop are:
1. To help you understand what sresss is.
2. To assist you in recognizing sources of stress in
    your life, including those that are personal and
    job related.
3. To provide you with an opportunity to plan manage-
    ment interventions to cope with these sources of
    stress.

"After completing this workshop you will have a beginning
knowledge of stress which you can utilize to design your own
personal stress management program.

10

"The design of the workshop takes a holistic approach to stress management and includes:

Definition of stress

Types of stress

Relaxation techniques

Stress diseases

Relationship of mind and body

Five stress management principles: time and energy management; improve your external environment; improve your internal environment; physical conditioning; nutrition awareness

Personal sources of stress

Job stress--symptoms, causes, cures

Development of a personal stress management plan."

II. SETTING OBJECTIVES

"At this point I would like to give people a chance to get to know others and to find out what others hope to gain from today's experience."

Option A--For Large Groups

"I'd like everyone to put on your name tag and stand up. Mill around silently and read as many name tags as you can while others are reading yours. When I say stop, form a group with two other people you do not know, and sit down together. When you are in threes, please count off one, two, three. Person one will begin by talking for one minute about any aspects of his or her name tag. When I call time, switch to person two. Person two then has one minute to talk, then person three."

Option B--For Small Groups

"I'd like everyone to put on his or her name tag and stand up. Mill around silently and read as many name tags as you can while others are reading yours. When I say stop, find one other person you do not know and sit in a pair facing each other. Assign yourselves letters A and B. Person A is to interview person B to determine why B came to the workshop, and what his or her goals are, that is, what B wants to learn from this group. Person A will have one minute for the interview. Then switch roles, with Person B interviewing Person A."

Go around the room having each person introduce his or her partner to the group, giving the partner's goals. Ask the partner if he or she wants to add anything to the goals. List name and goals for each person on the board or flipchart. Explain that you will compile goals for the group and give each person a list so that all will know what they set out to learn at the beginning of the workshop.

III. STRESS SIMULATION

"I would now like to take you through an exercise which should give you some indication of your own stress response. Settle back as comfortably as you can and close your eyes. (Ten second pause.) I would like you to recall a particularly stressful event which you have experienced. (Ten second pause.) Remember that stress can be anything from being hit by a brick to being addressed by a lover, from being hired to fired. (Ten second pause.) Remember the event. (Ten second pause.) The sights, the sounds, the tastes, the smells. (Ten second pause.) The feelings, the emotions, the thoughts. (Ten second pause.) The anger, the fear, the sadness, the elation. (Ten second pause.) Remember the person or persons involved. (Ten second pause.) Remember their reactions. (Ten second pause.) Remember their anger, their fear, their sadness, their elation. (Ten second pause.) Now continue to recall that situation in its entirety. (Ten second pause.) Soon, we will be going around the room and describing our respective situations. (Ten second pause.) Now monitor your reaction, both physical and emotional as I tell you that we shall not be sharing our situations. (Ten second pause.) Open your eyes."

Discuss the experience by asking the group the following questions: What were some of your responses to the exercise--your thoughts, feelings, physical reactions? How "real" was this exercise for you as a live experience of stress; did you respond as you usually do to stress?

IV. MINI-LECTURE: WHAT IS STRESS?

"Let's begin by finding out what you know already about identifying stress. I shall read a list of situations; please raise your hand if you would call any stressful:

- You just changed to a better job.
- You've been unemployed for over six months.
- You celebrate your fortieth birthday.
- Your first grandchild is born.
- You're finally taking that vacation you looked forward to all year.
- You've recently received a promotion.
- You scrape a fender on your new car.
- You slipped on the ice and sprained your ankle.
- Your dentist says you'll need some work done on your teeth.
- Your town has just been hit by a major snowstorm.
- You and your lover share a passionate kiss.

"As you can see from the group's responses, the nature of stress depends on how you see it. This is correct, as you'll discover when we look at what is known about stress."

Present the following mini-lecture in your own words. Utilize an outline of major points as a visual aid to your talk. It may be put on transparencies for use with an overhead projector or on a flipchart.

"Stress is a frequently used word that is not understood well. We often say that someone who is ill or having any other kind

of problem in life is 'under a lot of stress.' When we can't
identify the cause of our physical or emotional difficulties,
we are likely to say, 'It's all due to stress.' There may be
more truth in this than we realize, but it doesn't solve the
problem or cure the ailment if we stop there and don't try to
understand better what stress is all about. The growing interest in stress and in courses and workshops such as this reflects
the widespread awareness that stress is related to many physical
and mental disorders.

"I shall begin by defining stress and the components of stress
so that you can understand it more fully. This understanding
can lead to discovering ways to control stress instead of having
it control you. We shall then identify sources of stress in our
daily lives and learn effective ways for dealing with them.

"A growing body of knowledge about stress has been accumulating
over the past forty years, since Dr. Hans Selye first developed
a theory of stress.[2] Selye has spent most of his life conducting research on stress at the International Institute of Stress
at the University of Montreal. Many other physicians and psy-
chologists are conducting research on stress that is contribut-
ing to our understanding and has led to some promising methods
of stress management. What is most exciting and significant
for our well-being is that the stress researchers are providing
insights into how mind and body work together to produce

2. Hans Selye, The Stress of Life, rev. ed. (New York: McGraw-Hill
Book Co., 1978).

psychosomatic illness and how this knowledge can be used for prevention."

Definition of Stress: The General Adaptation Syndrome[3]

"An early definition of stress used by Selye is 'the rate of wear and tear within the body.'[4] Later, as a result of his research, Selye developed a more precise definition: 'Stress is the body's nonspecific response to any demand placed on it, whether or not that demand is pleasant.'[5] This definition is important because Selye discovered that the body always reacts in the same way to any kind of change. The change can be emotional or physical, painful, pleasant, or life threatening. The change for you could be traveling on vacation, losing your wallet, or cutting your finger. In all these situations we need to be able to meet the demands these changes put on us. Our bodies will always respond to these demands in three stages: the alarm reaction, resistance, exhaustion. This three-stage response is called the General Adaptation Syndrome, or GAS. It is our biological coping mechanism that prepares us for fight or flight."

Alarm Reaction

"In the alarm stage, the body recognizes the stressor, such as an attacking dog. Stress may also be emotional, such as dreading to visit a relative who is demanding and critical.

---

3. Ibid., p. 1.
4. Ibid., p. 65.
5. Ibid., p. 74.

"The body prepares for fight or flight by sending messages from the brain (hypothalamus) which stimulate the pituitary gland to release its hormones. These trigger the adrenal glands to pour out adrenaline. Adrenaline increases heartbeat and rate of breathing, raises blood sugar level, increases perspiration, dilates the pupils, and slows digestion. The process results in a huge burst of energy, greater muscular strength, and better hearing and vision that you can use to fight or run away."

Resistance
"In the resistance stage, the body repairs any damage caused by the stress and may adapt or get used to such stresses as extreme cold, hard physical labor, or worries. We learn to adapt or live with the stress.

"Most physical or emotional stressors are of brief duration so our bodies are able to keep up with the physiological demands of the stress. During our lifetime we go through the first two stages many times. We need these response mechanisms to adapt to the many demands of daily living and to protect us from more serious threats to our lives.

"However, if the stress continues without letup, the body must remain in a constant state of readiness for fight or flight and will be unable to keep up with the demands, leading to the stage of exhaustion."

Exhaustion
"Exhaustion usually affects only specific parts of the body and is temporary: runners in a marathon experience severe stress

in their muscles and cardiovascular systems, which leads to exhaustion, but after a good rest they are back to normal and are looking forward to the next race.

"If exhaustion continues without relief, you can develop one of the diseases of stress, such as high blood pressure, arterio-sclerosis, migraine headaches, gastrointestinal disorders, rheumatoid arthritis, or asthma. The body may even give up during this stage and die."

V. DEEP MUSCLE RELAXATION

A. Mini-lecture

"Deep muscle relaxation, or DMR, is a widely used technique to help people counteract and control bodily stress.[6] For those of us who suffer migraine or tension headaches, ulcers, backaches, hypertension, stiff necks, or tenseness elsewhere in our bodies (often set off by sitting most of the day or from under-use of our bodies), DMR can be a very helpful way to control stress.

"In the modern world, we need to learn to counteract some of our innate biological coping mechanisms in order to relax. The fight or flight response helped ancient man to survive, but today it is often counterproductive. The spurt of adrenaline, bracing of neck and back muscles, and quickened pulse that accompany sudden fear or anxiety usually have no appropriate physical outlet. It is socially unacceptable, for example, to run out of the room or to strike a person when we are upset, so we maintain an outward appearance of calm while clenching our teeth and suppressing our rage or fear. Because we are constantly exposed to stimuli that set off this survival reaction, we often feel tensed for flight or fight. The physical reaction we feel, when chronic, can lead to headaches, backaches, or other physical illnesses that are much more serious.

---

6. Edmund Jacobson, Progressive Relaxation (Chicago: University of Chicago Press, 1929).

20

"Unfortunately, many people use drugs, alcohol, or food to seek relief from this constant stress. We have become a nation of pill poppers, constantly faced with advertisements promising relief of backache or headache with pills or tranquilizers. Reliance on drugs is expensive, risky to our bodies, and can end in addiction. DMR is an alternative that will help you counteract the effects of bodily stress.

"DMR was developed in the 1930s by Dr. Edmund Jacobson, a clinical psychologist, who discovered that people can regulate certain effects of the autonomic nervous system through self-management techniques. In other words, you can learn to control your skeletal muscles and reduce levels of tension in those muscles. When we are keyed up by our biologic coping responses, we can, after practicing, consciously instruct our muscles to relax. When muscles are lengthened (in a state of relaxation), they cannot at the same time express tension; they cannot contract as they do in a fight or flight response. Anxiety and muscular relaxation produce opposite physiologic states, so one cannot be anxious when completely relaxed.

"Jacobson's technique simply involved learning to tighten and then relax the major muscles of the body. Practicing this daily teaches you to recognize what muscular tension feels like (the tensing) and to relax each muscle group in order to achieve total relaxation. After regular practice, you can voluntarily relax groups at will when you notice tenseness developing."

B. Exercise

Read the following script slowly, pausing about five to ten seconds between instructions. The script takes about twenty minutes to read.

"Practice while sitting in a chair. If you lie down, you may fall asleep, which is not the purpose of the exercise. The purpose is to teach you to make a conscious effort to relax. Your conscious awareness of bodily sensations of muscular tension and muscular relaxation is the key to success with this technique. With practice you will learn to relax tense muscles while going about your daily activities. If you ever do want to do the exercise lying down, to avoid stress to the lower back you should bend your knees. Anyone with lower back problems should consult a doctor before doing the part of the exercise that involved arching the lower back."

RELAXATION SCRIPT[7]

"Arms: Settle back as comfortably as you can. Let yourself relax to the best of your ability. Now, as you relax like that, clench your right fist. Just clench your fist tighter and tighter, and study the tension as you do so. Keep it clenched and feel the tension in your right fist, hand, forearm. Now relax. Let the fingers of your right hand become loose, and observe the contrast in your feelings.

---

7. Reprinted with permission from Joseph Wolpe and Arnold A. Lazarus, Behavior Techniques: A Guide to the Treatment of Neuroses (Oxford, England: Pergamon Press, 1966).

"Now, let yourself go and try to become more relaxed all over. Once more, clench your right fist really tight. Hold it, and notice the tension again. Now let go, relax; your fingers straighten out, and you notice the difference once more.

"Now repeat this with your left fist. Clench your left fist while the rest of your body relaxes; clench that fist tighter and feel the tension. And now relax. Again enjoy the contrast. Repeat that once more: clench the left fist tight and tense. Now do the opposite of tension: relax and feel the difference. Continue relaxing like that for a while.

"Clench both fists tighter and tighter: both fists tense, forearms tense. Study the sensations. Relax. Straighten out your fingers and feel that relaxation. Continue relaxing your hands and forearms more and more.

"Now bend your elbows and tense your biceps; tense them harder and study the tension feelings. All right, straighten out your arms; let them relax and feel that difference again. Let the relaxation develop. Once more, tense your biceps; hold the tension and observe it carefully. Straighten the arms and relax; relax to the best of your ability. Each time, pay close attention to your feelings when you tense up and relax. Now straighten your arms; straighten them so that you feel the most tension in the triceps muscles along the back of your arms; stretch your arms and feel that tension. Now relax.

"Get your arms back into a comfortable position. Let the relaxation proceed on its own. The arms should feel comfortably heavy as you allow them to relax. Straighten the arms once more so that you feel the tension in the triceps muscles; straighten them. Feel that tension, and relax.

"Now let's concentrate on pure relaxation in the arms without any tension. Get your arms comfortable and let them relax further and further. Continue relaxing your arms even further. Even when your arms seem fully relaxed, try to go that extra bit further; try to achieve still deeper levels of relaxation.

"Face, Neck, Shoulders, Upper Back: Let all your muscles go loose and heavy. Just settle back quietly and comfortably. Wrinkle up your forehead; relax and smooth it out. Picture the entire forehead and scalp becoming smoother as the relaxation increases. Now frown and crease your brows and study the tension; let go of the tension again. Smooth out the forehead once more.

"Now, close your eyes tighter and tighter. Feel the tension, and relax your eyes. Keep your eyes closed, gently, comfortably, and notice the relaxation. Now clench your jaws, bite your teeth together; study the tension throughout the jaws; relax your jaws now. Let your lips part slightly. Appreciate the relaxation. Now press your tongue hard against the roof of your mouth. Look for the tension. All right, let your tongue return to a comfortable and relaxed position. Now purse your lips. Press your lips together tighter and tighter; relax them. Note the contrast between the tension and your relaxation. Feel the relaxation all over your face, all over your forehead and scalp, eyes, jaws, lips, tongue, and throat. The relaxation progresses further and further.

"Now attend to your neck muscles. Press your head back as far as it can go and feel the tension in the neck; roll it to the right and feel the tension shift; now roll it to the left. Straighten your head and bring it forward; press your chin against your chest. Let your head return to a comfortable position, and study the relaxation. Let the relaxation develop. Feels good? Now shrug your shoulders, as tight as they will go. Hold the tension. Feel the pain. Drop your shoulders and feel the relaxation. Your neck and shoulders are relaxed. Shrug your shoulders again and move them around, loosely, easily, relaxed.

"Bring your shoulders up and forward and back. Feel the tension in your shoulders and in your upper back. Drop the shoulders once more, and relax. Pause to think; let the relaxation spread deep into the shoulders once more, and relax. Pause to think; let the relaxation spread deep into the shoulders, right into your back muscles. Feel a wave of peace spread through them. Let the relaxation spread deep into the shoulders, right into your back muscles. Relax your neck and throat and your jaws and the rest of your face. The pure relaxation takes over and grows deeper, deeper, ever deeper.

"<u>Chest, Stomach, Lower Back</u>: Relax your entire body to the best of your ability. Feel that comfortable heaviness that comes with relaxation. Breathe easily and freely, in and out. Notice how the relaxation increases as you exhale; as you breathe out, just feel the relaxation. Now breathe right in and fill your lungs; inhale deeply and hold your breath. Study the tension. Now exhale. Let the walls of your chest grow loose and push the air out automatically, Continue relaxing and breathe freely and gently. Feel the relaxation and enjoy it. With the rest of your body as relaxed as pos- sible, fill your lungs again. Breathe in deeply and hold it again. Fine. Let the air out and appreciate the relief. Just breathe normally. Continue relaxing your chest and let the relaxation spread to your back, shoulders, neck, and arms. Merely let go, and enjoy the relaxation.

"Now let's attend to your stomach area. Tighten your stomach muscles; make your abdomen hard. Notice the tension, then relax. Let the muscles loosen and notice the contrast. Once more, press and tighten your stomach muscles. Hold the ten- sion and study it, then relax. Notice the general well-being that comes with relaxing your stomach. Now draw your stomach in. Pull the muscles right in and feel the tension this way; now relax again. Let your stomach out. Continue breathing normally and easily and feel the gentle massaging action all over your chest and stomach. Again pull your stomach in and hold the tension. Now push out and tense like that. Hold the tension. Once more pull in and feel the tension; now relax your stomach fully. Let the tension dissolve as the relaxation grows deeper. Each time you breathe out, notice

the rhythmic relaxation both in your lungs and in your
stomach. Notice how your chest and your stomach relax more
and more. Try and let go of all contractions anywhere in
your body.

"Now direct your attention to your lower back. Arch up your
back, make your lower back quite hollow, and feel the tension along your spine. Settle down comfortably again, relaxing the lower back. Arch your body up and feel the tension
as you do so. Try to keep the rest of your body as relaxed
as possible. Try to localize the tension within your lower
back area. Relax once more, relaxing further and further.
Relax your lower back, relax your upper back, spread the
relaxation to your stomach, chest, shoulders, arms, and face.
All these parts relax further, and further, deeper, and
deeper.

"<u>Hips, Thighs, Calves; Complete Body Relaxation</u>: Let go of
all tensions and relax. Now flex your buttocks and thighs.
Flex your thighs by pressing down on your heels as hard as
you can; relax and note the difference. Straighten your
knees and flex your thigh muscles again. Hold the tension,
then relax your hips and thighs. Allow the relaxation to
proceed on its own. Press your feet and toes downward, away
from your face, so that your calf muscles become tense.
Study that tension; relax your feet and calves. This time,
bend your feet toward your face so that you feel tension
along your shins. Bring your toes right up; relax again.
Keep relaxing for a while. Now let yourself relax further,
all over. Relax your feet, ankles, calves and shins, knees,

thighs, buttocks, and hips. Feel the heaviness of your
lower body as you relax still further.

"Now spread the relaxation to your stomach, waist, lower
back. Let go more and more. Feel that relaxation all over.
Let it proceed to your upper back, chest, shoulders and arms,
and right to the tips of your fingers. Keep relaxing more
and more deeply. Make sure that no tension has crept into
your throat; relax your neck and your jaws, and all of your
facial muscles. Keep relaxing your whole body like that for
a while. Let yourself relax.

"Now you can become twice as relaxed as you are, merely by
taking in a really deep breath and slowly exhaling. With
your eyes closed, so that you become less aware of things
around you and thus prevent any surface tensions from developing, breathe in deeply and feel yourself becoming heavier.
Take in a long, deep breath and let it out very slowly. Feel
how heavy and relaxed you have become.

"In a state of perfect relaxation you should feel unwilling
to move a single muscle in your body. Think about the effort
that would be required to raise your right arm; see if you
can notice any tensions that might have crept into your
shoulder and your arm. Now you decide not to lift the arm
but to continue relaxing. Observe the relief and the disappearance of the tension; just carry on relaxing like that."
Pause for two minutes. "Now, I'd like you to think of an
imaginary scale from zero to one hundred, where zero is
complete relaxation and one hundred is maximum tension.

28

Consider approximately where you would place yourself on that scale, and remember the number so that you can jot it down after you have opened your eyes. I am going to count from five to one. When I reach the count of one, open your eyes, stretch, become wide awake. Five . . . four . . . three . . . two . . . one. Eyes open, wide awake."

Project the following scale on the screen with an overhead projector or draw on a flipchart.

RELAXATION SCALE

0	10	20	30	40	50	60	70	80	90	100

Ask the participants to tell you where they placed themselves on the relaxation scale and record their responses; then compute an average for the group. This gives you a sense of how effective the technique was for them and encourages them to practice on their own to achieve deeper levels of relaxation as a few individuals in the group may have done.

For those who had difficulty relaxing, encourage them to try practicing at home once a day. Improvement comes with practice. A tape cassette of one's own voice reading a relaxation script is helpful. Suggest that participants check their local libraries to locate the original Jacobson reference or find others they prefer. Relaxation recordings are often available at record stores. Give out "Summary of Deep Muscle Relaxation" (see page 31) and suggest they use it as a guide for practice. Explain further that once they learn to differentiate between feelings of tension and relaxation they can eliminate the tensing and focus entirely on relaxing their muscles. This is called progressive relaxation.

VI. HOME ASSIGNMENT

Suggest that group members try to practice DMR at least once daily (preferably twice daily for maximum benefit) in a quiet place, as far from distractions and interruptions as possible. It is best not to practice when very tired (to avoid falling asleep) and to take the telephone off the hook if possible.

Bring the session to a close by briefly asking for feedback on how participants liked Session 1, then announce next week's agenda.

HANDOUT FOR SESSION 1
SUMMARY OF DEEP MUSCLE RELAXATION

You can learn to relax all large muscle groups in your body. The method requires that you tense (tighten up and hold the tension) and then relax the muscle. Each time you do this, concentrate on the difference in body sensations and feelings between the tension and the relaxation. Learning these feelings will help you become aware of any tense muscles which you can then relax. The exercise progresses as follows:

   Right hand and forearm - twice
   Left hand and forearm - twice
   Biceps - bend elbow - once
   Triceps - arms stretched out - once
   Forehead - wrinkle up - once
   Forehead - wrinkle down - once
   Eyes - close tightly - once
   Tongue - pressed up to roof of mouth - once
   Neck - head pressed back - once
   Neck - head pressed back, rolling head to the left and to the
          right - twice
   Neck - chin pressed against chest - once
   Chest - deep breath, hold it, exhale slowly - twice
   Stomach - hold it in - twice
   Stomach - hold it out - twice
   Lower back - arch it up - twice
   Thighs - press down on heels - twice
   Calves - toes forward - twice
   Shins - toes up and back - twice

Try to practice this exercise two times daily for maximum benefit in a quiet place as free from distractions as possible.

SESSION 2
BRIEF OUTLINE

OBJECTIVES: To introduce any new members to the group.
                To introduce information about good and bad stress.
                To help group members identify stress in their lives.

   I. OPENING THE SESSION
      A. Objective
      B. Pregroup Session for New Members
      C. Introduction of New Members
      D. List of Objectives

  II. REVIEW OF HOME ASSIGNMENT

 III. GOOD AND BAD STRESS
      A. Exercise
      B. Mini-lecture
      C. Types of Stress--Exercise

  IV. RECOGNIZING STRESS IN OURSELVES
      A. Mini-lecture
      B. Exercise

   V. PRACTICE OF DMR
  VI. HOME ASSIGNMENT

      HANDOUTS

SESSION 2

I. OPENING THE SESSION

A. Objective
To introduce any new members to the group

B. Pregroup Session for New Members
In preparation, contact each of the people who did not attend Session 1 and ask them to meet with you fifteen minutes before the group begins Session 2. This pregroup meeting gives you an opportunity to meet with the new group members and discuss the goals and purpose of the workshop. Briefly go over the material covered in Session 1 and give them the handout for the session. Explain that the group developed a set of goals for the workshop and that you will ask each of them to add their goals to the list at the beginning of the session.

C. Introduction of New Members
1. Option for Small Groups: Have a quick go-round, everyone giving names. Ask the new participants to introduce themselves to the group, explaining who they are and what they want to get out of the workshop.
2. Option for Large Groups: Explain that there are a few new people who missed the first session, and ask the new people to introduce themselves and give a brief statement about what they want to get out of the workshop.

D. List of Objectives

As the new members are introduced, add their objectives to the list the group made in Session 1. Tell the group that a complete list of the objectives will be distributed at Session 3.

II. REVIEW OF HOME ASSIGNMENT

Ask for comments and feedback from participants on their experience with the practice of deep muscle relaxation which they were assigned for homework. Encourage people to find the time to practice DMR in order to reduce the negative effects of their physical response to stress.

III. GOOD AND BAD STRESS

A. Exercise

"Let's take a few minutes now to find out what kinds of activities or situations you experience as good stress or bad stress."

1. Distribute copies of "Some Good and Bad Stress for Me" (see page 43).
2. Ask participants to think of three stresses or situations that cause bad stress for them and three that are good. Allow about two minutes.
3. Ask volunteers to share their good and bad stressors. List the responses on a flipchart or chalkboard. The differences and similarities in the group's perceptions of stress and an awareness of choice in how they perceive stress should emerge.

B. Mini-lecture

"Is all stress bad? A life without stress would be pretty dull. Stress can add excitement to life. It is impossible to live without experiencing some degree of stress all the time. Even when we are asleep our bodies are functioning; dreaming produces some stress. We would have to be dead to be free of all stress. Looking back at the list of situations you consider stressful, we can see that each item is potentially stressful. Some might be considered bad stressors--they can cause damage or distress-- and others are obviously pleasurable. When you embrace your lover you feel your pulse race, your breathing speed up, and your heart pound. Would you want to give up this

pleasure? Most of the other situations are subject to
your own interpretations. Not everyone perceives the
same situation in the same way, so what is stressful for
me may not be stressful for you.

"A key idea Hans Selye presents is that 'what matters is
not so much what happens to us, but the way we take it.'[1]
Herein lies the key to stress management and a concept
that relates to psychosomatic medicine. We will make use
of this important principle when I introduce you to some
techniques for reducing the stress reaction.

"Selye believes that a certain amount of stress is needed
for well-being. He calls this positive stress. The
body's stress response mechanism can stimulate us enough
so we can achieve peak performances for important jobs.
You can probably recall times when you 'came through'
despite minor illness or low energy. We hear of people
performing amazing feats of strength in emergency situa-
tions--such as lifting a car from a person trapped be-
neath. Other examples of positive stresses are a date
with someone new, an infant learning to walk, a student
facing an exam, a job interview. We grow excited and
tense while watching our favorite team in a play-off
match. Pleasurable emotions produce feelings of
exhilaration. These positive stresses put less demand on
the body than do negative stresses, for reasons not yet

1. Hans Selye, The Stress of Life, rev. ed. (New York: McGraw-
Hill, 1978).

36

understood. They energize us and produce healthy relaxation.

"Selye calls the kind of stress that can be harmful 'distress.' Distress results when the stress continues so that we need to keep adapting to it. If the distress continues long enough, it can result in exhaustion. Some examples of distress are: serious illness of self or family member; lack of sleep; relationship problems with spouse, family, friends; worries about money, family; bottled-up feelings such as intense anger, fears, frustrations. Long-term distress can contribute to the development of migraine headaches, peptic ulcers, heart attacks, hypertension, mental illness, and suicide.

"Most of the stressors we encounter are emotional stressors. The stressor effect depends more on how we react to the stress and less on what caused it. Each of us has developed ways of reacting to the various stressors we encounter. It is this conditioned response that can create problems and possible threats to our health. It can help us learn how to manage stress if we first identify some of the common stressors most of us have to deal with at some time."

C. Types of Stress--Exercise
The purpose of the exercise is to increase the participants' awareness of the broad range of stressors that everyone experiences throughout the life span.

Page 44 of the handout section is a chart listing types
of stress. This chart can be used in two different
ways:

1. You can present the material on the chart as a brief
    lecture, give the group copies of the chart, and
    have them suggest examples or additions.

2. You can divide the group into four subgroups. As-
    sign each of the groups one category of life
    stressors--1. life-cycle stressors, 2. social stress,
    3. physical and personal stress, and 4. job stress.
    Ask each group to select a recorder and compile a
    list of stressors for their category.

    Allow five minutes for the subgroups to complete
    their lists.

    Have the recorder from each subgroup read their list
    and put the results on a flipchart or chalkboard.
    After all of the groups have recorded their lists,
    reform the larger group and ask participants to make
    any additions that were overlooked.

IV. RECOGNIZING STRESS IN OURSELVES

A. Mini-lecture

"Stress in one area of our lives such as in a relationship or on the job cannot be understood and managed without considering the many other sources of stress we cope with every day. Stress cannot occur in isolation from all the many other stressors we have to deal with. If you hope to succeed at reducing stress from one specific source such as the job, it will be helpful to begin by making a personal assessment of stress in all areas of your life. You may be facing such major stressors as loss of income, serious illness, death of a family member, change in residence or birth of a baby, plus a multitude of comparatively minor stressors both positive and negative. These major and minor stressors have a cumulative effect and, added together, make up your total stress-adaptation score. Your stress score can vary from year to year depending on the number of changes in your life.

"Each of us has personal stress-adaptation limitations. When you exceed this level, stress overload may lead to poor health or illness. To avoid exceeding your personal limits, learn to heed the warning signals from your body and mind that tell you when stress levels are getting too high. When you observe warning signs such as feeling tense and keyed up, having difficulty sleeping, frequent headaches and indigestion, it is time to take preventive action. Consider postponing another major change if possible. Ask yourself, 'Am I ignoring my rising level of discomfort as I pile on more responsibility and change?'

"A tool we shall use that will enhance self-awareness about the sources of stress in life is the Life Change Test, a brief inventory of life events developed by Dr. Thomas Holmes and his associate, Richard Rahe.[2] Holmes and Rahe studied the relationship of common life changes to the onset of serious illness. They assigned a numerical score from one to one hundred to each of these events according to the degree of adaptive energy required to cope with each change. The total life-change score was found to be predictive of the chances of developing serious physical or mental illness in the near future."

B. Exercise
1. Give out copies of the inventory, "How Much Stress Is In Your Life?" (see handouts, pages 45-46). Instruct participants to score themselves by checking only those events which they experienced in the past year. This should take about five minutes.
2. Ask them to form groups of three to share their reactions to the questionnaire and any ideas they have about coping. Allow five minutes.
3. Reassemble the group and inquire about participants' reactions to the questionnaire and what they learned. Emphasize that having a high or low score does not

---

2. Thomas Holmes and Richard H. Rahe, "Social Readjustment Rating Scale." Journal of Psychosomatic Research 11 (1967): 213.

guarantee that a person will develop an illness or remain healthy. Probabilities are not people; each person will react uniquely. However, it would be wise for those who got high scores to consider the possibility of reducing additional sources of stress; for those who got low scores, there is risk in assuming it is acceptable to pile on the stress indefinitely.

V. PRACTICE OF DMR

A. Introduction

"Before we begin, I'd like each of you to think back on last week's session and the practicing you have been doing at home. Which areas of your body were most difficult to relax? Was it the back of the neck, forehead, temples, stomach, lower back, thighs, or some other area? Usually the spots that are hardest to relax are where you will first notice tension. It is important to identify your primary tension spot so that you can learn to monitor and control stress. For example, if your neck is hardest to relax, you will want to try to be conscious of when your neck feels tense.

"Tension is like an alarm that tells you it is time to relax because your level of stress is building. After practicing DMR with the tensing of muscles, eventually you will be able to produce a relaxed muscle state without tensing and be able to tune in to a troublesome spot and relax it at will."

B. Practice

Read the relaxation script from Session 1 (see pages 22-29).

Record relaxation levels achieved on the Relaxation Scale
from Session 1.

VI. HOME ASSIGNMENT

"Continue to practice DMR one or two times daily, being aware
of tension spots. practice an abbreviated from of DMR during
the day when you notice tension spots getting tight by closing
your eyes and trying to relax your entire body while thinking,
'My neck is completely relaxed, my neck is completely relaxed,'
until you feel the muscles relax.

"Once during the week go through the DMR routine without
tensing while saying to yourself silently, 'My right hand is
completely relaxed,' and so on. If you find this difficult,
practice again with the tensing and relaxing method and then
try to do it again without the tensing."

42

HANDOUTS FOR SESSION 2
SOME GOOD AND BAD STRESS FOR ME

Write in the space below three stressors you encounter frequently that are good for you and three that are bad.

Good Stress	Bad Stress
1.	1.
2.	2.
3.	3.

TYPES OF STRESS

LIFE CYCLE

Infancy

Childhood

Adolescence

Marriage

Pregnancy

Parenthood

Job demands

Divorce

Empty nest

Death of spouse, family
member, other

Senior years

PERSONAL

Attitudes about yourself
like/dislike, capable/
incapable

Feelings - anger, fear,
anxiety

Expectations of others
friendly/hostile,
helpful/harmful

SOCIAL

Inflation/recession

Technological unemployment

Urban problems

Changing values

Energy crisis

Relocation

Travel

JOB

Job dissatisfaction

Conflict - with supervisors,
co-workers

Work overload

Monotony

Time pressures

Unclear expectations

Public attitudes

PHYSICAL

Disability

Illness

Injury

Addictions

HOW MUCH STRESS IS IN YOUR LIFE?

Score yourself on this Life Change Test.* Check only those events which you have experienced in the past year.

Item No.	Item Value	Happened ( )	Your Score	Life Event
1	100	_____	_____	Death of spouse
2	73	_____	_____	Divorce
3	65	_____	_____	Marital separation
4	63	_____	_____	Jail term
5	63	_____	_____	Death of close family member
6	53	_____	_____	Personal injury or illness
7	50	_____	_____	Marriage
8	47	_____	_____	Fired at work
9	45	_____	_____	Marital reconciliation
10	45	_____	_____	Retirement
11	44	_____	_____	Change in health of family member
12	40	_____	_____	Pregnancy
13	39	_____	_____	Sex difficulties
14	39	_____	_____	Gain of new family member
15	39	_____	_____	Business readjustment
16	38	_____	_____	Change in financial state
17	37	_____	_____	Death of close friend
18	36	_____	_____	Change to different line of work
19	35	_____	_____	Change in number of arguments with spouse
20	31	_____	_____	Mortgage over $10,000
21	30	_____	_____	Foreclosure of mortgage or loan
22	29	_____	_____	Change in responsibilities at work
23	29	_____	_____	Son or daughter leaving home
24	29	_____	_____	Trouble with in-laws
25	28	_____	_____	Outstanding personal achievement
26	26	_____	_____	Wife begins or stops work
27	26	_____	_____	Begin or end school
28	25	_____	_____	Change in living conditions

* Thomas H. Holmes and Richard H. Rahe, "The Social Readjustment Rating Scale," Journal of Psychosomatic Research 11 (1967): 213-18, reprinted with permission.

Item No.	Item Value	Happened ( )	Your Score	Life Event
29	24	_____	_____	Revision of personal habits
30	23	_____	_____	Trouble with boss
31	20	_____	_____	Change in work hours or conditions
32	20	_____	_____	Change in residence
33	20	_____	_____	Change in schools
34	19	_____	_____	Change in recreation
35	19	_____	_____	Change in church activities
36	18	_____	_____	Change in social activities
37	17	_____	_____	Mortgage or loan less than $10,000
38	16	_____	_____	Change in sleeping habits
39	15	_____	_____	Change in number of family get-togethers
40	15	_____	_____	Change in eating habits
41	13	_____	_____	Vacation
42	12	_____	_____	Christmas
43	11	_____	_____	Minor violations of the law

Total Score for 12 Months _____

The more change you have, the more likely you will suffer a decline in health. Of those who scored over 300 "life change units," 80% have a chance of a serious health change. With 150-299 life change units, about 50% get sick in the near future. With less than 150 life change units, about 30% get sick in the near future.

SESSION 3

BRIEF OUTLINE

OBJECTIVES: To introduce information about stress-related
              diseases, the diseases of the twentieth century.
              To help participants identify signs of stress
              in themselves.
              To teach and practice the relaxation response.

   I. OPENING THE SESSION--HOME ASSIGNMENT REVIEW

  II. MINI-LECTURE--DISEASES OF THE TWENTIETH CENTURY

 III. WAYS WE EXPRESS STRESS
      A. Introduction
      B. Exercise Instructions

  IV. THE RELAXATION RESPONSE
      A. Mini-lecture
      B. Practice of Relaxation Response

   V. STRESS MANAGEMENT PRINCIPLE 1--TIME AND ENERGY
      MANAGEMENT

  VI. HOME ASSIGNMENTS

      HANDOUTS

SESSION 3

I. OPENING THE SESSION

Inquire about the participants' success with the DMR home
assignment. Ask if they have identified tension spots and
whether they were able to relax without tensing by repeating
the phrase, "My . . . are completely relaxed." Encourage regular practice to improve their ability to relax tensions at will
and reduce stress.

Distribute the list of group objectives for the workshop and
discuss it briefly.

II. MINI-LECTURE: DISEASES OF THE TWENTIETH CENTURY

"The science of medicine has conquered many of the major infectious diseases that were fatal in the past for huge numbers of people. Sometimes, entire communities were wiped out. The western world has witnessed the disappearance of cholera, typhoid, smallpox, and more recently, diphtheria, whooping cough, measles, and polio. Success in eradicating these diseases is a result of medical technology and research. Medical researchers studied the causes of these diseases and developed methods to destroy the micro-organisms involved.

"At the same time, there is an enormous increase in deaths from diseases related to psychological and environmental factors. These are the stress-related disorders--the major diseases of twentieth-century society--cardiovascular disease, cancer, arthritis, respiratory disease.[1] Stress-related disorders or psychosomatic disease is terminology that is used interchangeably and refers to mental or physical malfunction or damage that results from the combined effects of a negative stressor and a maladaptive emotional response.

"These diseases are not conquered easily, because the causes are extremely complex. They are not caused by micro-organisms that can be controlled or eliminated by developing antitoxins.

---

1. Kenneth Pelletier, Mind as Healer, Mind as Slayer (New York: Delacorte Press, 1977), pp. 156-157.

"Although it may take many more years before we learn how to control the diseases of our modern society, evidence is accumulating that stress plays a crucial role.

"Our ability to cope with these diseases as a society and as individuals is hampered by our attitudes and beliefs about why we get sick.[2] The way we react to our own illnesses, and the way we are treated by our doctors and others when we get sick, is to assume that something foreign has made us sick. To get well again we need only to take the right medicine, allow ourselves to receive proper care, and give up our personal and social responsibilities until the disease-causing factors are vanquished. This is essentially a passive approach to regaining health. It is how we respond when germs are the culprits--we view ourselves as victims, powerless without the skill of the physician. We hold these beliefs and adopt the role of victim to our own detriment when we face stress-related disorders.

"We've learned that it is socially acceptable to be physically ill because of the generally accepted belief that we cannot help it. For some of us, the benefits of illness become so attractive that unconsciously we program our bodies to make us sick or to prolong or prevent recovery. Perhaps as a child you discovered that you could stay home from school or avoid facing some event if you had a stomachache and your mind and

---

2. Dennis T. Jaffe, Healing From Within (New York: Knopf, 1980).

body cooperated and worked together to bring on an actual upset stomach.

"Three factors that lead to stress disease have been identified:[3] (1) Stress that continues unabated or is extreme and is more than the body can handle leads to (2) Changes in the nervous system and the body organs, including reduction of white cells and suppression of the immune system, creating conditions for disease. Genetic predisposition may determine vulnerable spots. (3) A high concentration of life-change events. When this combination of factors occurs, there is a likelihood that disease will develop. In addition, there is evidence that certain personality styles should be included as a fourth factor that contributes to stress disease.

"Researchers have been looking into the possibility that there may be a link between personality, emotions, and the onset of stress disease. There is no question that personality influences the way that we react to stress. In childhood, we learn through trial and error and by watching parents, teachers, and other people how to deal with stressful situations. Our past successes, failures, rewards, and punishments may still determine how we handle stress in daily life. If we are lucky, how we learned to perceive and react to stress in the past is still functional and effective today. Most of us, however, did not learn in childhood how to manage the stress we face as adults.

---

3. Pelletier, Mind as Healer, pp. 117-19.

"Some individuals have developed personality styles and de-
fenses that may contribute to stress disease. We may feel
so fearful of making mistakes, of being criticized, of doing
less than a perfect job that we withdraw from challenging
situations or avoid confrontations, which results in feeling
unfulfilled, frustrated, incompetent. As children, we may
have learned that expressing feelings--especially anger--can
get us into trouble. We express our anger indirectly or deny
it altogether. We may develop headaches or indigestion
instead.

"Many women, and people in jobs such as nursing, teaching, the
human services, and others who provide direct services to
individuals may neglect their own need for caring and affec-
tion by taking care of others, while hoping to get approval
and love in this way. Such nonassertive personality styles
will increase the level of stress in an individual's personal
life and on the job by allowing stress to build and failing to
take action to reduce it.

"The largest body of evidence linking style of response to
stress with a specific disease is the research of Meyer
Friedman and Ray Rosenman, two cardiologists who first de-
scribed Type A behavior and concluded that it is a major cause
of coronary heart disease.[4] They found Type A behavior pattern
to be more predictive of coronary heart disease than the standard risk factors, such as a high fat diet and lack of exercise.

---

4. Meyer Friedman and Ray H. Rosenman, Type A Behavior and Your
Heart (New York: Fawcett Crest Books, 1974).

"They describe Type A behavior as characterized by a competitive, aggressive, achievement-oriented, time-dominated orientation to life. Type A people are usually unaware that their behavior creates problems for others or is detrimental to their health and well-being, since this behavior is condoned and applauded by our achievement-oriented society.

"Type A men and women share two common traits: (1) excessive competitive drive, which is present in all areas of their lives --they have a drive to excel in everything they do; and (2) chronic time urgency--they are continually driven by the clock, by having to meet deadlines; they are obsessed by numbers; they try to do more and more at a faster and faster pace; they are running on an accelerating treadmill of their own making.

"Many Type As also exhibit free-floating hostility, especially toward other competitors or people and situations that slow them down. A slow driver poking along in front of him or her can arouse a Type A's hostility to a fever pitch.

"Type As have a hard time relaxing. Weekends, vacations, free time with family and friends cannot be enjoyed, because the Type A, obsessed by work and the need to achieve and accumulate things, is busy worrying about the time spent being nonproductive. Type As will not allow themselves the leisure to develop hobbies or new interests. When they talk, which is usually much of the time, they finish sentences for others, interrupt often, hurry them along. To make a point, Type As raise their voices, talk louder and faster, and do not take the time to be good listeners. Type As have trouble coping with change and stress and feel insecure if they do not have full control over the people and events in their lives. Type As see their lives as a constant struggle, so they keep their arteries and bodies in overdrive to cope with the unending tasks and challenges they create for themselves. All these personality characteristics make the Type A person vulnerable to stress disease.

"The behavior of a Type B person, in contrast, is everything Type As reject. Type Bs have found a comfortable, more relaxed cruising speed at which to travel through life. They look at scenery with enjoyment, allow time for frequent refreshment and rest stops, really enjoy being alone or with friends and family. Type Bs work more slowly and thoughtfully, which can permit greater creativity. They allow themselves the leisure to develop more fully as people, and have to have a number of interests, activities, and friendships outside of work. Many Type Bs have plenty of drive, some are heads of corporations, but time is scheduled with a calendar, not a stopwatch. Type Bs have learned how to enjoy life.

"Most people do not have all the characteristics of the Type A pattern at all times, but if you recognize any of them in yourself or suspect that you are moving in that direction you should consider modifying your life-style.

"With regard to other stress-related diseases such as cancer, arthritis, asthma, ulcers, and migraine headaches, the research connecting personality factors with these diseases is inconclusive. There is an urgent need to study the relationship that exists between personality factors and illness. The underlying causes of any specific disease are extremely complex, and will probably always include physical, emotional, and environmental factors.

"Assessment of your individual risk factors needs to be conducted and evaluated by a skilled clinician; the average person lacks the experience and knowledge to make such a judgment. However, by increasing your awareness of the many factors that may contribute to the diseases of modern society, you can begin taking preventive action before symptoms develop. Consultation with your physician can help you evaluate and modify your life-style and improve your general health in order to minimize the effects of stress in your life and reduce the risks of stress-related disease."

III. WAYS WE EXPRESS STRESS

A. Introduction

"Is there any way that each of us can tell whether we have experienced more stress than our bodies can handle? Hans Selye has identified a list of symptoms and behaviors that are fairly reliable indicators that we are suffering from distress.[5] This list of danger signs is not meant to increase stress by raising your anxiety level about your state of health, but to serve as a signal to take some preventive action. Instead of waiting to become sick, we can learn to recognize signs of severe stress and take steps to remove the source of stress or reduce the stress reaction. In this way we can take active responsibility for our health and prevent many stress-related illnesses."

B. Exercise

Give each participant a copy of "Self-Observable Signs of Stress" (see pages 64-65). Have participants check off the ways they express stress and circle the reaction to stress that gives the most difficulty or the one that occurs most often. Allow about five minutes for participants to do this.

C. Discussion

Discuss participants' reactions to the checklist. When leading this discussion, explain that you are not asking

---

5. Hans Selye, The Stress of Life, rev. ed. (New York: McGraw-Hill, 1978), pp. 174-77.

56

that they reveal personal symptoms, but what they learned in general about how they usually express stress. That is, did they discover they express stress mainly through their bodies, their minds, their feelings, or all three? Close the discussion by underscoring the importance of being alert to signs of stress overload such as those in this listing so that they can take early action to reduce the stress and prevent illness.

IV. THE RELAXATION RESPONSE: MEDITATION

A. Mini-lecture

"The relaxation response is a simple, mental nonreligious meditation technique. It is a scientific method of working with the consciousness, which entails concentration of attention and awareness on a single idea, object, or point inside or on the body through repetition of a sound, word, or phrase. The physiological and psychological effects of the relaxation response counteract the body's flight or fight response.

"When practiced systematically for fifteen to twenty minutes twice daily, the relaxation response has a significant effect on stress and its side effects. People who meditate regularly have a lowered metabolic rate (blood pressure drops points, which can reduce borderline hypertension to a normal range); show a marked decrease in the use of alcohol, drugs, and cigarette smoking; show improved ability to deal with stress, and increase their sense of well-being. Meditation has also been found to enhance empathy, to sharpen mental processes, and to correlate with various measures of enhanced interpersonal functioning.

"It is not hypnosis, which is always goal directed--for example, stopping smoking. This alteration in consciousness involves a qualitative and quantitative change in mental alertness and visual imagery. These changes in turn produce deep rest and restoration of functioning by interrupting the adverse stimuli that set off the fight or flight response.

"The relaxation response procedure was developed by Dr. Herbert Benson, a Harvard cardiologist who studied the physiological responses to all types of meditation (including Hindu, Buddhist, transcendental meditation, and Zen) and determined the basic elements necessary to produce relaxation."

Benson's Relaxation Technique[6]

"The basic technique for eliciting the relaxation response is extremely simple. Its elements have been known and used for centuries in many cultures throughout the world. Four basic elements are common to all these practices: a quiet environment, a mental device, a passive attitude, and a comfortable position. A simple, mental noncultic technique based on these four elements follows:

"A quiet environment: One should choose a quiet, calm environment with as few distractions as possible. Sound, even background noise, may prevent the elicitation of the response. Choose a convenient, suitable place--for example, a quiet room where you will not be interrupted.

---

6. Herbert Benson, The Relaxation Response (New York: William Morrow, 1975), pp. 112-115. Reprinted with permission of the publisher.

"A mental device: The meditator employs the constant
stimulus of a single-syllable sound or word. The syllable
is repeated silently or in a low, gentle tone. The purpose
of the repetition is to free oneself from logical,
externally-oriented thought by focusing solely on the
stimulus. Many different words and sounds have been used
in traditional practices. Because of its simplicity and
neutrality, the use of the syllable 'one' is suggested.

"A passive attitude: The purpose of the response is to
help one rest and relax, and this requires a completely
passive attitude. You should not scrutinize your performance or try to force the response, because this may well
prevent the response from occurring. When distracting
thoughts enter the mind, they should simply be disregarded.

"A comfortable position: The meditator should sit in a
comfortable chair in as restful a position as possible.
The purpose is to reduce muscular effort to a minimum.
The head may be supported; the arms should be balanced or
supported as well. The shoes may be removed and the feet
propped up several inches, if desired. Loosen all tight-
fitting clothing."

B. Practice of Relaxation Response
    Read the following script and tell participants that they
    will receive a copy so they can practice at home.

    "In a quiet environment, sit in a comfortable position.

"Close your eyes.

"Deeply relax your muscles, beginning at your feet and progressing up to your face: feet, calves, thighs, lower torso, chest, shoulders, neck, head. Allow them to remain deeply relaxed.

"Breathe through your nose. Become aware of your breathing. As you breathe out, say the word 'one' silently to yourself. Thus: breathe in, breathe out, with 'one.' In, out with 'one.'

"Continue this practice for five minutes. You may open your eyes to check the time, but do not use an alarm. When you finish, sit quietly for several minutes, first with your eyes closed and then with your eyes open.

"Do not worry about whether you are successful in achieving a deep level of relaxation; maintain a passive attitude and permit relaxation to occur at its own pace. When distracting thoughts occur, ignore them and continue to repeat 'one' as you breathe. The technique should be practiced once or twice daily. Wait at least two hours after any meal, since the digestive processes seem to interfere with the elicitation of the expected changes.

"When practicing at home, continue breathing in and out with 'one' for twenty minutes. We have shortened the time here to permit us to go on to other things."

Record the participants' relaxation level on the relaxation scale in Session 1.

V. STRESS MANAGEMENT PRINCIPLE 1--TIME AND ENERGY MANAGEMENT

"Awareness precedes change. By now we have begun to know more about what causes stress, what it is, and some techniques we can use to manage it. There are other things that we can do to reduce stress in our lives.

"The first principle of stress management on which we shall concentrate is managing how we spend our energy and time. Energy and time management will help us handle stress more effectively. Before we can change our use of time and energy, however, we have to evaluate what we presently do that may be causing us stress. Most of us waste huge amounts of time and energy daily and are not even aware that we are doing it. The first step then toward effective time and energy use is to see where we are now through a self-assessment exercise."

A. Exercise on Energy Management
   1. Distribute the "Self-Assessment Sheet on Energy Use" (see page 66) and pencils. Give participants five to seven minutes to complete the questions.

   2. Ask the participants to form pairs with persons whom they do not know well. One at a time, they are to share with their partners the bad habit that they wish to change and the price they pay for it. The partner is to listen and then both of them are to brainstorm together ways to change the habit and form an action

62

plan for change. Allow about five minutes for each partner to have a turn.

3. In the same pairs, have each partner choose one person, place, thing, or activity that is a stressor that he or she would like to change. Have the partners, one at a time, share the stressor and brainstorm with each other to form an action plan to deal with the stressor. Allow about five minutes for each partner to have a turn.

4. Reassemble the entire group and ask if members would like to share what they learned about coping with one of their stressors or a high stress habit.

VI. HOME ASSIGNMENT

1. Hand out the summary of the relaxation response (see pages 67-68) and ask group members to try to practice the relaxation response once or twice daily (before meals if possible).

2. Ask participants to try to carry out the action plans they developed for changing bad habits or stressors during the week.

HANDOUTS FOR SESSION 3
SELF-OBSERVABLE SIGNS OF STRESS*

_____ 1. General irritability, hyperexcitation, or depression

_____ 2. Pounding of the heart, an indicator of high blood pressure

_____ 3. Dryness of the throat and mouth

_____ 4. Impulsive behavior, emotional instability

_____ 5. The overpowering urge to cry or run and hide

_____ 6. Inability to concentrate, flight of thoughts and general disorientation

_____ 7. Feelings of unreality, weakness, or dizziness

_____ 8. Predilection to become fatigued, and loss of the "joie de vivre"

_____ 9. "Floating anxiety" (We are afraid although we do not now exactly what we are afraid of.)

_____ 10. Emotional tension and alertness, feeling of being "keyed up"

_____ 11. Trembling, nervous ticks

_____ 12. Tendency to be easily startled by small sounds, etc.

_____ 13. High-pitched, nervous laughter

_____ 14. Stuttering and other speech difficulties

_____ 15. Bruxism, or grinding of the teeth

_____ 16. Insomnia

---

* Adapted with permission of the publisher from Hans Selye, The Stress of Life, rev.ed. (New York: McGraw Hill, 1978), pp. 174-77.

_____ 17. Hyperactivity (A tendency to move about without any reason, an inability to just take a physically relaxed attitude, sitting quietly in a chair or lying on a sofa.)

_____ 18. Sweating

_____ 19. The frequent need to urinate

_____ 20. Diarrhea, indigestion, queasiness in the stomach, and sometimes vomiting

_____ 21. Migraine headaches

_____ 22. Premenstrual tension or missed menstrual cycles

_____ 23. Pain in the neck or lower back

_____ 24. Loss of or excessive appetite

_____ 25. Increased smoking

_____ 26. Increased use of legally prescribed drugs, such as tranquilizers or amphetamines

_____ 27. Alcohol and drug addiction

_____ 28. Nightmares

_____ 29. Neurotic behavior

_____ 30. Psychoses

_____ 31. Accident proneness

SELF-ASSESSMENT SHEET ON ENERGY USE

1. A bad habit I would like to change is . . .

2. The price I pay for that habit in discomfort, stress, and lack of enjoyment of life is . . .

3. Type A (high stress) habits I have (check your habits)

   _____ Speaking fast
   _____ Constant competition
   _____ Ignoring or denying tiredness
   _____ Setting quotas
   _____ Doing two things at once
   _____ Pretending to listen
   _____ Overscheduling
   _____ Clenching fists or jaws

4. My stressors

   People _____

   Places _____

   Things _____
     or
   Activities _____

66

BENSON'S RELAXATION TECHNIQUE*

The four basic elements are:

A quiet environment: Choose a quiet, calm environment with as few distractions as possible. Sound, even background noise, may prevent the elicitation of the response. Choose a convenient, suitable place--for example, a quiet room where you will not be interrupted.

A mental device: Employ the constant stimulus of a single-syllable sound or word. The syllable is repeated silently or in a low, gentle tone. The purpose of the repetition is to free oneself from logical, externally oriented thought by focusing solely on the stimulus. Many different words and sounds have been used in traditional practices. Because of its simplicity and neutrality, the use of the syllable "one" is suggested.

A passive attitude: The purpose of the response is to help one rest and relax, and this requires a completely passive attitude. You should not scrutinize your performance or try to force the response, because this may well prevent the response from occurring. When distracting thoughts enter the mind, they should simply be disregarded.

A comfortable position: The meditator should sit in a comfortable chair in as restful a position as possible. The purpose is to reduce muscular effort to a minimum. The head may be supported; the arms should be balanced or supported as well. The shoes may be removed and the feet propped up several inches, if desired. Loosen all tight-fitting clothing.

---

* Adapted with permission from the publisher from Herbert Benson, The Relaxation Response (New York: William Morrow, 1975).

PRACTICE OF THE RELAXATION RESPONSE

· In a quiet environment, sit in a comfortable position.

· Close your eyes.

· Deeply relax your muscles, beginning at your feet and progressing up to your face: feet, calves, thighs, lower torso, chest, shoulders, neck, head. Allow them to remain deeply relaxed.

· Breathe through your nose. Become aware of your breathing. As you breathe out, say the word "one" silently to yourself. Thus: breathe in, breathe out, with "one." In, out, with "one."

· Continue this practice for twenty minutes. You may open your eyes to check the time, but do not use an alarm. When you finish, sit quietly for several minutes, first with your eyes closed and then with your eyes open.

Do not worry about whether you are successful in achieving a deep level of relaxation, maintain a passive attitude and permit relaxation to occur at its own pace. When distracting thoughts occur, ignore them and continue to repeat "one" as you breathe. The technique should be practiced once or twice daily. Wait at least two hours after any meal, since the digestive processes seem to interfere with the elicitation of the expected changes.

SESSION 4

BRIEF OUTLINE

OBJECTIVES: To continue self-assessment in time and energy management.
To learn about matching stress management methods with types of stress.

I. OPENING THE SESSION--HOME ASSIGNMENTS REVIEW

II. STRESS MANAGEMENT PRINCIPLE 1--TIME AND ENERGY MANAGEMENT

A. Time Management Exercise--Time Pies

III. MINI-LECTURE--MATCHING STRESS MANAGEMENT METHODS WITH TYPES OF STRESS

IV. DETERMINING A STRESS MANAGEMENT METHOD FOR YOUR TYPE OF STRESS

V. PRACTICE OF RELAXATION RESPONSE

VI. HOME ASSIGNMENT

HANDOUTS

SESSION 4

I. OPENING THE SESSION

   A. Relaxation Response Practice
   Inquire about participants' success with the relaxation
   response. Encourage group members to help each other with
   suggestions. Allow three to five minutes for feedback and
   sharing.

   B. Progress in Action Plans
   Have the pairs who worked together last week get back
   together to discuss their progress in putting their action
   plans to work. Partners should work together to revise
   plans as necessary. Allow about ten minutes.

II. STRESS MANAGEMENT PRINCIPLE 1--TIME AND ENERGY MANAGEMENT

"We shall continue our self-assessment today by looking at how we actually spend our time now and at how we might spend it more meaningfully and less stressfully. The following exercise will help you analyze whether there is a healthy balance between work and play in your life. It will help you see what activities are most meaningful to you, and how you can fit those into your daily schedule."

A. Time Management Exercise--Time Pie[1]
   1. Objective
      To emphasize inventory as a way of looking at your life more closely because self-assessment is the first step to action.

   2. Instructions
      a. Distribute copies of the handout "Time Management-- Time Pies" (see page 82) or 5" x 8" index cards and put instructions, questions to be answered, and a sample time pie on a flipchart or chalkboard. Allow about twenty minutes for group members to complete their time pies.
      b. Instruct each group member to draw a time pie and divide it into sections allotting slices according to the amount of time and energy he or she spends

---

1. Exercise adapted from Sid Simon, Meeting Yourself Halfway (Niles, Ill.: Argus Communications, 1974). Used with permission.

on each activity in an average week (forty-five
percent work, ten percent social, ten percent
sleep). This chart is to cover all primary commitments and answer the question, "How many hours do
you spend on the following": sleeping; at work, on
the job; on work you take home; with friends;
alone pursuing a hobby; reading or watching television; on chores around the house; with the
family; on miscellaneous activities?

SAMPLE TIME PIE--AVERAGE WEEK

c. When the group members have completed their pies,
have them answer the following questions:
Who are the significant others in each slice?

Would you like to change the various slices of your pie? For example, do your real interests lie where your time and energies are now invested?

List the most important people in your life drama. Rank according to the time and energy you invest in them. Do they invest the same amount in you?

d. Now have each member draw a "perfect pie" of his or her life, indicating how large he or she wants each activity slice to be. Then ask, "What might you actually do to change the size of the various slices to make them more 'perfect' for you?"

3. Discussion

a. When participants have completed the time pie exercise, have them form groups of three.

b. Have each person in the smaller groups discuss any aspect of the exercise for five minutes.

c. Reassemble the whole group and ask that participants share some of what they did in their sub-groups. Statements beginning "I learned . . ., I discussed . . ." and so on are helpful.

III. MINI-LECTURE--MATCHING STRESS MANAGEMENT METHODS WITH TYPE OF STRESS

"Individuals vary in how they respond to the tension of daily life. What is stressful for one person may not distress another. Further, people do not respond to stress in the same ways.

"Some of us express stress physically; we may develop headaches, hypertension, or ulcers. Others have trouble concentrating, feel their mind racing, or experience emotional reactions such as increased anxiety or fearfulness, depression, or obsessive negative thoughts. One way to counteract the effects of stress is through relaxation. Edmund Jacobson, developer of deep muscle relaxation, sums it up as follows: 'Anxiety and tension are incompatible with physical and mental relaxation. If a person lets himself relax, he can control or block the anxiety, tension, or fears.'[2]

"Certain methods work best to reduce bodily stress symptoms while others combat mental and emotional stress symptoms. The basic principles to guide us in choosing the best methods for us are: Self-regulation of behavior (including voluntary focusing of attention) in a given mode (physical or mental) to reduce or inhibit unwanted activity in that specific mode. And, self-regulation of behavior in a given

---

2. Edmund Jacobson, _Progressive Relaxation_ (Chicago: University of Chicago Press, 1929).

74

mode (physical or mental) may, to a lesser degree, reduce unwanted activity under other modes.[3]

"In other words, we need to identify how we respond to stress (physically or mentally or both) and then pick a method that works directly on that mode. Procedures that affect bodily tension directly reduce physical stress most effectively; techniques that result in changes in mental events are most effective with mental and emotional stress."

Distribute copies of the handout, "Types of Stress and Suggested Relaxation Techniques for Each" (see page 83), so that participants can jot down notes while you talk.

"I would like each of you to close your eyes and recall the last time you felt distressed. Try to recall how you reacted to that stress. Decide if it was primarily a physical or mental reaction. Many of us, when under intense stress, react both physically and mentally, but most of us favor one mode or the other. When you have a good idea of your usual mode of expression, open your eyes.

"I am going to review three modes of reacting to stress and describe some methods that work well for each mode. Be thinking about which method might suit your needs."

---

3. Richard J. Davidson and Gary E. Schwartz, "Matching Relaxation Therapies to Types of Anxiety: A Patterning Approach," in Relax: How You Can Feel Better and Reduce Stress and Overcome Tension, ed. John White and James Fadiman (New York: The Confucian Press, 1976),p. 191.

Physical

"The first mode of reacting to stress is with our bodies. The following techniques are for those people who suffer physical symptoms--headaches, backaches, stiff necks, tense or rigid bodies, ulcers, high blood pressure.

"Deep Muscle Relaxation (DMR) is a technique that we have already discussed. It was developed by Edmund Jacobson and is especially good for high somatic and low cognitive stress. DMR is a passive process that involves focusing attention on the various gross muscle groups throughout the body. First you tense, then release each group of muscles while thinking, 'relax, relax, relax,' to build up an association between mental process and physical relaxation. Practicing DMR builds up somatic cues so that eventually an automatic relaxation response will take place when one thinks, 'Relax.'

"Progressive Relaxation is a similar technique, except that you do not tense your muscles. Instead, you mentally suggest relaxation by thoughts like, 'My feet are completely relaxed, my feet are completely relaxed,' while consciously relaxing foot muscles. Progressive relaxation is often accompanied by deep breathing or visualization techniques, and may be used as a warm-up exercise to systematic desensitization.

"Autogenic Training is a passive somatic attention technique involving leaning back in a comfortable chair in a quiet room.[4] With eyes closed, you use verbal formulas to make mental contact with parts of your body. For example, you might say to yourself, 'My arm is getting warm and heavy'; you will then feel relaxed with a warm, heavy arm. There are a series of steps to learn in order to use this method effectively. Essentially, it involves meditating about a somatic event in order to produce somatic change.

"Hatha Yoga, an ancient system of self-development, leads to physical and mental calmness and is good for controlling moderate somatic and cognitive stress. It includes physical exercises and relaxation as well as breathing techniques, nutrition, and concentration.

"Massage involves active somatic techniques that can help you achieve a good balance between relaxation and stimulation, rest and activity. Self-massage can improve posture and circulation, and make you aware of the tensions and stresses that build up in your body over the day. Massage directly relaxes muscle tension.

"Deep Breathing Exercises can reduce tension by producing a deep state of calmness and relaxation. When you breathe softly and slowly, it is difficult for your emotions to become aroused out of a tranquil state. Several disciplines include breathing exercises as part of their relaxation strategies. In yoga, 'pranayama,' or control of the life force, is an

---

4. Patricia Carrington, Freedom in Meditation (New York: Doubleday, 1978), pp. 25-27.

important study. Since we all must breathe anyway, breath control is a quick and simple way to relieve tension and increase energy.

"Exercise is extremely important for well being. Unlike machines, our bodies are made for activity. Long life and health are promoted by regular exercise of the body. If we do not exercise, we tend to atrophy. We become more suscep- tible to disease and less able to combat stress."

Psychological

"The second mode of reacting to stress is with our minds. The following techniques are for those who suffer mental symptoms--worry, obsessive thoughts, mind-racing, inability to concentrate.

"Meditation--The relaxation response is another technique we have covered. Developed by Herbert Benson, meditation works best on low cognitive and somatic stress and is especially useful for people with borderline hypertension.[5] It involves regulating your attention to produce a state of general auto- nomic quiescence. If attention is focused on a mantra or scene, it will reduce stress more effectively than if atten- tion is focused on a bodily process such as breathing.

"Hatha Yoga promotes mental and spiritual pacification. Re- laxation, deep breathing exercises, and concentration aim to

---

5. Herbert Benson, The Relaxation Response (New York: Morrow, 1975).

78

reduce tension, overcome fear, and produce feelings of inner peace and tranquility.

"Deep Breathing with Visualization involves imagining a pleasant scene or image while relaxing through deep breathing. The visualization blocks other mental activity and reduces stress.

"Progressive Relaxation with Mental Focus and Visualization involves focusing on the words 'calm' and 'relaxed' while breathing deeply--'calm' on inhale and 'relaxed' on exhale-- or visualizing a relaxing scene (lying on a beach, sitting in a tranquil forest); can produce mental relaxation.

"Active Generation of Cognitive Behavior requires that you distract your mind from worry or distress by focusing on a mentally demanding game or other activity to reduce mental stress.

"Involvement of Entire Perceptual-Cognitive System such as watching television or a movie, or reading a book, which we commonly refer to as 'escape' activities, are ways of diverting attention from adverse stimuli and resting the mind.

"Activities such as dancing, walking, and sports involve us mentally and physically and can relieve stress by diverting attention from our problems while maintaining our physical health.

"Systematic Desensitization is a set of procedures designed to treat problems associated with inappropriate conditioned anxiety. The steps involve: (1) deep muscle relaxation; (2) establishing a scale of subjective anxiety responses; (3) constructing a hierarchy of anxiety-provoking stimuli; and (4) simultaneously maintaining the relaxed state and imagining anxiety-associated stimuli from the hierarchy. This procedure enables people to learn a new response to a stimulus that previously was associated with fear. It is especially useful for specific phobias, performance anxiety, and other problems of malconditioning.

"Hypnosis is an active cognitive process that attempts to reduce anxiety by the active generation of mental behavior. It involves shifting attention and generating imagery."

Physical and Psychological

"The third mode of reacting to stress is with mind and body.

"Vigorous Physical Exercise is effective in combatting stress because it demands active physical and mental attention and, therefore, reduces both modes of stress. Tennis, jogging, biking, hiking, swimming, martial arts, sports such as basketball and volleyball--all demand physical and mental involvement that prevent symptoms from appearing at the same time."

IV. DETERMINING A STRESS MANAGEMENT METHOD FOR YOUR TYPE OF STRESS

Ask participants to look over the handout "Types of Stress and Suggested Relaxation Techniques for Each" and check which type of stress they experience the most and then check one method listed that they are willing to try during the week.

V. PRACTICE OF THE RELAXATION RESPONSE

Read the relaxation response script form Session 3 (see pages 60-61). Record participants' levels of relaxation achieved on the relaxation scale from Session 1.

VI. HOME ASSIGNMENT

A. Encourage participants to continue to practice the relaxation response one or two times each day.

B. Participants should find out more information on the stress management techniques that they chose in the exercise--where yoga classes meet, a book on meditation, where they can play tennis, and so on.

HANDOUTS FOR SESSION 4

TIME MANAGEMENT--TIME PIES

1. Assess how you spend your time:

   Sleeping

   At work, on the job

   On work you take home

   With friends

   Alone pursuing a hobby

   Reading, watching TV

   Chores at home

   With the family

   Miscellaneous activities

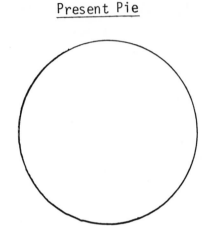

Present Pie

2. Answer the following questions:

   List the significant people in each slice.

   Is time spent on your real interests?

   List the most important people in your life. Rank according to time you invest. Do they invest the same amount in you?

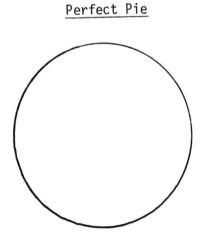

Perfect Pie

3. Draw your "perfect or ideal" pie. What might you actually do to change the size of the various activity slices to make them more "perfect" for you?

TYPES OF STRESS AND SUGGESTED RELAXATION
TECHNIQUES FOR EACH

A. <u>Physical--Bodily or a Somatic Stress</u>

Deep muscle relaxation

Progressive relaxation

Autogenic training

Meditation on bodily focus (breathing)

Hatha Yoga

Massage

Deep breathing exercises

Exercise

B. <u>Mental--Cognitive Stress</u>

Meditation (relaxation response format)

Hatha Yoga

Deep breathing with visualization

Progressive relaxation with cognitive focus and visualization

Active generation of cognitive behavior (playing chess, etc.)

Involvement of entire perceptual-cognitive system (watching TV
or a movie, reading)

Activities (dancing, walking, sports)

Systematic desensitization

Hypnosis

C. <u>Combination of Physical and Mental Stress</u>

Vigorous physical exercise--jogging, running, biking, hiking,
swimming, tennis, martial art forms, basketball, volleyball

Any activity that demands one's concentrated physical and mental
attention

SESSION 5

BRIEF OUTLINE

OBJECTIVES: To assist participants to identify sources of stress
in their external environment, including stress on
the job.
To assist them to develop better ways of managing
that stress.

I. OPENING THE SESSION--HOME ASSIGNMENTS REVIEW

II. STRESS MANAGEMENT PRINCIPLE 2--IMPROVE YOUR
ENVIRONMENT

III. STRESS ON THE JOB

   A. Sources of Job Stress
   B. Job Stress Profile
   C. Coping with Job Stress
   D. Exercise

IV. PRACTICE OF RELAXATION RESPONSE

V. HOME ASSIGNMENT

   HANDOUTS

I. OPENING THE SESSION--HOME ASSIGNMENTS REVIEW

Inquire about members' success with the relaxation response practice. Solicit thoughts and opinions from others who practiced during the week or answer questions yourself.

Ask volunteers to share what they found out about the stress management technique they investigated last week. You may want to put some of the information on a flipchart.

II. STRESS MANAGEMENT PRINCIPLE 2--IMPROVE YOUR ENVIRONMENT

TAKE MORE CONTROL OF WHAT AND WHO ARE SURROUNDING YOU AND HOW YOU INTERACT WITH YOUR ENVIRONMENT

A. <u>Exercise</u>
1. Distribute copies of "Improving My External Environment Worksheet" (see page 97) and pencils. Allow five minutes for participants to fill them in.

2. Break the group into subgroups of three persons. Each person is to share responses for one minute with his or her partners, then the subgroups should spend two minutes on feedback or suggestions.

3. Reassemble the group and ask about reactions to the worksheet.

"The worksheet will help you see that you can take steps to make your environment less stressful and to increase your ability to cope with stresses. Reducing unnecessary noise

and irritations, getting the rest you need, and antici-
pating and planning for upcoming changes or crises enable
you to exert more control over what is surrounding you.

"Another way to improve the environment is by improving
how you relate to that environment. People are an
important part of our surroundings, so taking steps to
relate better to others through more open and honest
communication makes living more pleasant. Building a
support system of friends also reduces stress, as friends
provide security, companionship, and positive strokes when
we need them. Build a positive cocoon around yourself by
establishing a comfortable home atmosphere; redecorate
and put yourself into your surroundings, so that when you
come into your apartment or house it feels homey and warm.
You can do the same at work with plants or pictures and
by adding personal touches to your workplace.

"What are some of your ideas of things you can do to
improve your environment?"

Allow two or three minutes for feedback from entire
group.

III. STRESS ON THE JOB

"Stress in the workplace has received considerable attention in the last few years. There has been a steady flow of articles in newspapers and magazines and television features about the danger of stress in general, and of stress on the job in particular to our physical and mental health.

"Stress on the job can lead to serious, life-threatening illness and even violence. In 1968, a worker in Michigan shot and wounded eighteen co-workers because he was upset about being called names. We do not usually become violent when our jobs become stressful, but we also usually do not even acknowledge that we feel stressed on the job until we reach the exhaustion stage when we might explode in anger, develop a serious emotional problem, or get sick. Job stress can result in heart disease, ulcers, emotional disability, absenteeism, poor job performance, and high turnover rates.

"A major research study on job stress sponsored by the National Institute for Occupational Safety and Health analyzed symptoms of stress in 130 different jobs in the state of Tennessee between 1972-1974.[1] Data was collected from three sources: death statistics, hospital admissions, and mental health center admissions. The psychologically related illness found most frequently was digestive system problems--

---

1. Wayne C. Richard, Ronald D. Fell, and William L. Wallace, "How Stressful is Your Job?" (Nashville, Tenn.: Dede Wallace Center, 1978), pp. 3, 5, 7, 12.

gastritis, duodenitis, ulcers. Second was circulatory system problems, including hypertension. The leading cause of premature death was heart disease. The results of the study identified a group of ten occupations that were most stressful. These occupations in rank order are: 1. inspectors, 2. warehouse workers, 3. public relations workers, 4. clinical lab technicians, 5. machinists, 6. laborers, 7. guards and watchmen, 8. sales managers, 9. mechanics, 10. structural metal craftpersons.

"Also high on the list were miners, painters, waiters and waitresses, nurses aides, practical nurses (LPN), health technicians, policemen, carpenters, electricians, office managers, dietitians, and managers and administrators. The researchers pointed out that these occupations will not always be the most stressful jobs in Tennessee, or in any other location, and they do not know the extent to which nonjob-related stress contributed to the illness in these workers. More research is needed to answer the question of how much job stress directly causes physical or mental illness in comparison to other sources of stress.

"Most managers are aware of the threat to health and safety that environmental hazards on the job create and try to eliminate or prevent dangerous working conditions. But little is being done by most employers to understand and change the negative psychological effects of work stress. The concept of stress in the workplace is a new idea that is slowly gaining acceptance. A few organizations recognize that stress is a costly problem and are beginning to help workers control job stress by setting up preventive programs. These preventive programs include psychological counseling, workshops to stop smoking and control stress, and employee fitness facilities. In the meantime, most of us will have to rely on our own individual efforts to cope with stress on the job.

"Why has management of stress in the workplace not yet become a top priority for everyone? Lack of progress in controlling stress on the job, despite rapid advances in technology in other areas, can be attributed to an acceptance of the goals of our achievement-oriented society, fueled by the Western work ethic which keeps us tied to the productivity treadmill. These values also explain why many people will overlook or minimize the symptoms of stress until they can no longer be ignored. Society acts as if it believes that idle hands are indeed the devil's workshop; therefore, we suffer pangs of guilt if we dare to put our own personal well-being ahead of our job. Some of us apply this philosophy to every aspect of our life and even work hard at playing and relaxing --to set aside a couple of days of unscheduled idleness is tainted with wickedness.

"When we go to work, no one is surprised when the manager seems to care mainly about how completely we can commit ourselves to the job. Central issues at the workplace usually are how much we can produce, how many widgets we can make, how much service we can provide, how many people we can take care of, and how much overtime we can work--with or without extra pay. The message we get from most organizations, even before we start to work, is: 'Expect to be stressed.' The thinking

seems to be that no self-respecting organization or employee
would want it any other way. Without realizing it, workers
and managers hold mutual beliefs about work that can set up
the conditions for high levels of job stress. Furthermore, if
both you and your employer expect work to be stressful and
accept it simply as a fact of life, neither of you will
probably think about giving much time and energy to managing
job stress. The end result will be that both managers and
workers will continue to drive themselves while ignoring
feelings of stress, until they break down in physical or
mental illness."

A. Sources of Job Stress

"What are some of the common job stressors we all experience? Researchers have identified these:[2]

"Role Ambiguity. There is confusion about what your
work objectives are; you are not sure what your specific
tasks are--what you will and will not be doing. There is
no job description.

"Role Overload or Underload. Tasks are too easy or too
difficult. You are given too much or too little to do.

"Role Conflict. Your job consists of conflicting demands
--performance of one task may interfere with another, such

---

2. J.R.P. French, Jr., and R.D. Caplan, "Organizational Stress and
Individual Strain," in The Failure of Success, ed. A.J. Marrow
(New York: American, 1972).

90

as in relationships with people or how time and resources
are spent. You feel pressured to fulfill conflicting
expectations; there are differences with supervisors.

"Responsibility for People. You are responsible for the
work of others, their careers, advancement, job security,
or compensation.

"Low Participation. You do not have much control over
your work; you do not have a choice of tasks or input
into how work is supervised and training is planned. You
are unable to influence how decisions are made that affect
your work. Studies demonstrate that having control over
what one does is essential for job satisfaction.

"Where does job stress come from? Sources of job stress
can be found anywhere in the total work environment.
Some job stressors are:
    work overload
    time pressure, deadlines
    conflict with supervisors
    conflict with co-workers
    job dissatisfaction
    unclear job expectations
    job monotony
    promotion or increased responsibility--especially
        difficult when the person promoted is lacking
        new skills needed and is not given training to
        prepare for the job
    technological change and threat of job loss

dead end jobs

hazardous work requiring a state of hyperalert-
    ness, such as police, firemen, bus and cab
    drivers, hospital staff, air-traffic controllers,
    structural steel workers

lack of recognition

negative public attitudes

no control over your job

unfair treatment in pay and job status

noisy, crowded workspace."

B. Job Stress Profile

1. Distribute copies of "Job Stress Profile" (see page
   98) and ask participants to complete the profile.
   You will use it as a basis for discussion; they can
   take it home and use it in developing their own
   personal plan for coping with stress on the job.
   Allow five minutes, but extend time if needed.

2. Ask the group to give examples from their work stress
   in their own jobs; list on a flipchart or chalkboard.
   Add sources of stress they might have overlooked.
   Identify the most common as well as unique stressors,
   by a show of hands. Ask participants to identify
   sources of stress they think are primarily internal
   sources of stress, that is, stress that originates
   within the individual, such as difficulty being
   assertive with a supervisor. Ask them to identify
   those that are external sources of stress, such as a
   noisy, crowded workplace. In this discussion, point

92

out that, in many situations, both internal and external sources of stress will contribute to the overall level of stress experienced. In devising stress management strategies, it is helpful to know which components of stress have internal causes; they may have more control over such causes and could begin by finding ways to reduce these internal sources.

3. Ask the group to list symptoms of stress. Add any that they omitted. Point out that symptoms are useful as signals that let us know when stress levels are too high and tell us we should take immediate steps to reduce stress. Attitudes of toughing it out or ignoring symptoms are not helpful and put us at risk of stress disease.

C. Coping with Job Stress

"The biggest problem in coping with job stress is not an inability to identify the problems or lack of resources. It is an unwillingness to take the time to give to yourself, whether that time be spent in relaxation, in establishing a new set of work habits, or in making a change in your own life-style. What can you do once you are aware that you are suffering job stress? A successful program would include:

"Identify. Identify the kinds of stress you experience, when do they occur; how frequently; who or what is involved? What do you do to increase stress at work?

93

"Prioritize. Rank for immediate attention those stresses which bother you the most (intensity, frequency). Choose ones to work on where change is possible.

"Past Coping. What coping methods have you tried in the past; with what success, failure?

"Consideration of Solutions. Which solutions can be implemented with most ease? Which are more difficult or risky to carry out? Who can help you to achieve your goal?

"What do we want from our jobs? Many people want more job satisfaction, more opportunities to learn and grow, a chance to use talents and skills, and more sense of doing something that really matters.

"If you are experiencing job stress, you undoubtedly have some of the same desires that are not being fulfilled. Therefore, it will be important for you to assess your job situation and find ways to get more of what you want from your work."

D. Exercise
   1. Distribute copies of the worksheet, "Coping with Job Stress" (see page 99). Ask participants to take five minutes to complete it as best they can in this limited time. Give examples of how to answer the questions. Explain that they should plan to give

more time and thought to this task on their own at
home.

2. After they have completed the worksheet, ask them to
    find a partner and take five minutes to share any
    aspect of their responses.

3. Reassemble the large group and ask volunteers to
    share their experience with the exercise: what they
    learned or discovered; coping ideas they wish to
    try or offer to the group.

Point out that to be successful in managing job stress,
participants should plan to assess periodically their
sources of job stress and their success with coping efforts, in order to ensure focus on the true sources of
stress and to utilize the optimum coping means available.
Warn them that when they stop making assessments of job
stress and their progress in dealing with it, they are in
danger of trouble. If they find that job stress continues
after they have allowed a reasonable time to carry out a
coping method, then it is time to reassess the stress and
their methods.

IV. PRACTICE OF RELAXATION RESPONSE

Read the relaxation response script from Session 3 (see pages 60-61). Record class levels of relaxation achieved on the relaxation scale from Session 1.

V. HOME ASSIGNMENT

1. Distribute copies of "25 Ways of Combating Job Stress" (see pages 100-101). Discuss the material on the sheet with the participants, encourage them to add any ideas they might have to the list.

2. Ask participants to look again at the "Job Stress Profile" that they completed earlier in the session. Direct their attention to question five: "One step I will take the next working day to reduce job stress for me." Ask them to put their plan into action the next working day. They should write down their feelings and results. Encourage participants to try some of the ideas on the list "25 Ways of Combating Job Stress," during the week and record their results.

HANDOUTS FOR SESSION 5

IMPROVING MY EXTERNAL ENVIRONMENT
WORKSHEET

1. One way I can reduce unnecessary noise and irritations around me is to:

2. The amount of sleep I need each day in order to be maximally alert and able to cope with stress is:

3. I presently get that amount of sleep or rest.

   Yes _____   No _____

4. (For those who answered No to #3):

   A way I could rearrange my schedule in order to get enough sleep is:

5. Some changes or crises I foresee over the next year are:

6. Ways I can deal with these stresses are:

JOB STRESS PROFILE

1. Some sources of job stress for me are:

2. Clues that reveal to myself and others that job stress is an important stress factor in my life:

3. How I now cope with job stress:

4. Some ideas or new ways to cope with job stress I want to try:

5. One step I will take the next working day to reduce job stress for me:

98

COPING WITH JOB STRESS

1. <u>Identify</u> kinds of stress you experience.

    When does it occur?

    How frequently?

    Who or what is involved?

    Any bad habits involved?

2. <u>Prioritize</u> which job stresses bother you most.

    Choose one to work on first.

3. <u>Review</u> coping methods you've tried with what success, failure?

4. <u>Consider possible solutions.</u>

    Which can be implemented with most ease?

    Who can help with implementation?

25 WAYS OF COMBATING JOB STRESS

Here are some ways to cope with job stress you might consider trying. Begin with the easier and simpler ones first to build your confidence before you embark on a more ambitious program of changes.

1. Start off your day with breakfast, at home or on your way to work.

2. Occasionally change your routine by meeting a friend or co-worker for breakfast--allow enough time to really enjoy it.

3. Avoid drinking coffee or soft drinks all day; drink water or fruit juice instead.

4. Organize your work--set priorities.

5. Write it down, don't overburden your memory.

6. Don't try to be perfect, to do everything right at all times.

7. Don't try to do two or three or more things at once.

8. Consider occasionally coming in earlier or staying later instead of taking your work home with you every night.

9. Reduce the noise level if possible. Rugs, draperies can help in an office.

10. Restrict telephone calls by having them held or close the door when you are extra busy or need to concentrate.

11. Consider planning to use uninterrupted blocks of time which may actually save time and tempers for big jobs or a collection of smaller jobs.

12. Create a pleasant work environment in your immediate surroundings insofar as possible.

13. Speak up about petty annoyances while respecting the other's feelings.

14. Develop co-worker support networks. Can peak workloads be shared?

15. Don't take your job with you on breaks.

16. Take a creative lunch break. How much of the city or area within lunch time radius of your job have you ever really explored?

17. Occasionally go out to lunch with a co-worker or friend.

18. Take a ten or twenty-minute meditation break during lunch hour, or a yoga or exercise break.

19. Optimize your health with good nutrition, exercise, sleep, and rest.

20. Monitor your work, rest, recreation balance. Are changes needed?

21. Develop with co-workers your own brand of happy hour or celebrate birthdays or other events as a break in the routine.

THE FOLLOWING REQUIRE MORE EFFORT BUT WILL HAVE LONG-TERM PAY-OFFS

22. Develop a wider variety of sources of gratification in your life, family, friends, hobbies, interests. Plan occasional special weekends or mini-vacations.

23. Consider changing your job or having your job responsibilities changed to better meet your interests and skills.

24. Be assertive, learn how to express differences, make requests and say "no" constructively. Consider taking a course in assertive training.

25. Don't overlook the emotional resources available to you that are close at hand--co-workers, supervisor, spouse, friends. This suggestion needs to be underscored for the male sex, who are programmed by society to avoid discussing or acknowledging feelings and problems but pay for it in stress disease.

SESSION 6

BRIEF OUTLINE

OBJECTIVES: To assist participants to identify sources of stress in their internal environments and to assist them to develop better ways of managing that stress. To introduce information on physical conditioning as it relates to stress management.

I. OPENING THE SESSION--HOME ASSIGNMENT REVIEW

II. STRESS MANAGEMENT PRINCIPLE 3--IMPROVE YOUR INTERNAL ENVIRONMENT

III. STRESS MANAGEMENT PRINCIPLE 4--BUILD UP YOUR STAMINA AND RESISTANCE TO STRESS THROUGH PHYSICAL CONDITIONING

IV. PRACTICE OF DEEP MUSCLE RELAXATION

V. HANDOUTS AND HOME ASSIGNMENT

SESSION 6

I. OPENING THE SESSION--HOME ASSIGNMENT REVIEW

Ask the participants to form groups of three and to share what
they did during the week to reduce job stress and how successful
they were. They will discuss what they did and then receive
feedback and suggestions of new methods from their partners.
Each person in turn will speak and receive feedback and
assistance for five minutes. Allow about fifteen minutes.

Reassemble the group and ask volunteers to share the steps they
took to reduce job stress and how effective they were. You
might inquire whether any others tried the same approach and
with what success. Ask whether talking over their stress reduction efforts with others in this exercise was helpful.

Some participants may need support to continue working on finding an effective stress reduction method for their job. Allow
about fifteen minutes for group discussion.

II. STRESS MANAGEMENT PRINCIPLE 3--IMPROVE YOUR INTERNAL
ENVIRONMENT

A. Exercise
Distribute copies of "Improving My Internal Environment
Worksheet" (see page 112) and pencils. Allow five
minutes for participants to fill them in. Explain that
this worksheet will not be shared and is solely for awareness purposes.

B. Mini-lecture
Before beginning the mini-lecture distribute copies of
"Steps Toward Improving Your Internal Environment" (see
page 113).

"We can improve our internal environment by training and
shaping our minds. Loosening up inhibitions, overcoming
our limitations, and working on developing a positive
attitude toward life are all important aspects of a well-
rounded, stress-controlled existence.

"As I go over the following coping strategies, I would
like you to be thinking of your responses on the worksheet
and how you can use these strategies to help you deal with
the stressful people, places, and things and worries you
listed there.

"Develop a positive attitude toward life. Put stressors in
a favorable context. If you can convince yourself that
some stress is useful or necessary, you will reduce the

effects of stress. In other words, recognize the beneficial aspects of stress, even to the point of seeking growth lessons in bad experiences. Use the power of positive thinking; your attitude determines whether you perceive any experience as pleasant or unpleasant.

"Learn to take it easy. Many of us take things too seriously and need to learn to take one thing at a time. When we worry too much we need diversion, something to put in the place of worrying--a pleasant thought, a thought stoppage (a technique to stop negative thought patterns by shouting words like 'stop' or 'no' in the middle of an anxious series of thoughts), or a change of scene (getting away from a painful situation in order to catch your breath and give yourself a new perspective-- going to a movie, reading, visiting a friend, doing something to escape from your routine). Remember, 'Worry is like rocking in a rocking chair. It gives you something to do, but gets you nowhere.'

"Set aside quieting time. Practice the relaxation response or deep muscle relaxation. Regulating the activity of your mind or body will reduce unwanted activity in that mode. Practicing meditation with visualization helps reduce worrying and anxious thoughts; DMR helps reduce tension in the body.

"Talk out your worries with a friend or a professional if you are preoccupied with emotional problems. This helps clarify problems and control anxiety. Therapy, by helping you relax and become aware of your feelings and behavior, helps you remain calm in otherwise anxious situations.

"Set your goals on inner peace and serenity. We all need to learn to accept what we cannot change, to learn to love ourselves, and not to be afraid. Instead of worrying about the past or the future, focus on living in and enjoying the present with an attitude of gratitude for the chance to be alive. By accepting your limits and choosing beliefs that help you deal with the unknowable, you can feel a sense of purpose and inner peace.

"Educate your mind. Improve your ability to cope with stress by reading about human growth, stress, and the dimensions of life; arm yourself with knowledge."

C. Discussion
Lead a brief discussion on the strategies for coping with internal stress. Have any of the participants used any of these methods and if so, how effective was it for them? Does anyone have other coping strategies to suggest?

III. STRESS MANAGEMENT PRINCIPLE 4--BUILD YOUR STAMINA AND RESISTANCE TO STRESS THROUGH PHYSICAL CONDITIONING

A. Mini-lecture

"Why do we need to exercise? 'Inactivity is a serious health hazard, linked to hypertension, chronic fatigue, physiological inefficiency, premature aging, poor musculature, and inadequate flexibility.'[1] Exercise is 'the key element to long life' because it protects us by preventing or reversing physical illness, reduces physical tension and anxiety, and increases the quality of our lives. Our bodies, unlike machines, atrophy from lack of use and need frequent exercise to stay in tune. For most people in today's world, our daily rounds do not provide enough physical activity to meet that need. Today's American is alienated from his or her body; forty-five percent of us do not exercise at all and lead a sedentary life, which is known to be one of the risk factors that lead to high blood pressure and heart disease.

"The Framingham Heart Study found that the death rate from cardiovascular and coronary heart disease was seven times greater for the most inactive men than for the most active

---

1. Donald B. Ardell, High Level Wellness: An Alternative to Doctors, Drugs, and Disease (New York: Bantam, 1979).

men.[2] Regardless of the presence of other risk factors
such as middle age, high blood pressure, and cigarette
smoking, the researchers reported that people who are
sedentary are at greater risk.[3] Without regular exercise
we risk shortening our life span. Regular exercise can
prevent premature death and promote our general well
being. The researchers strongly recommend that we build
into our daily activities some vigorous exercise to
counteract the effects of our modern society that encourages a sedentary life-style. They add two important
cautions: 1. Strenuous exertion by a middle-aged, overweight, sedentary person can be hazardous. For such
persons, a medical evaluation is essential before beginning
an exercise program. 2. Exercise alone will not reduce
risk of coronary heart disease. What may be even more
important for you may be to give up smoking, control your
blood pressure, or modify your diet.[4]

"There are other benefits of exercise. Regular sessions
of physical conditioning that push your heart and lungs
toward their capacity through gradual continuous exercise
not only increase the efficiency of body delivery of

2. William B. Kannel, "Recent Findings from the Framingham Study-
1," Medical Times (April 1978): 3-4.
3. William B. Kannel and Paul Sorlie, "Some Health Benefits of
Physical Activity," Archives of Internal Medicine 139 (August 1979):
859-60.
4. William B. Kannel et al., "Physical Activity and Coronary Vulner-
ability: The Framingham Study," Cardiology Digest 6 (1971): 39.

oxygen to the tissues, but also develop new growth of capillaries to carry more blood to the muscles. This causes a lowering of heart rate and blood pressure, a reduction of body fat (helps control overweight), and increased ability to deal with stress. Exercise builds strength, flexibility, and endurance, which make us more resistant to fatigue, able to do work, and take sudden stress. It also enables us to recover more quickly from illness and accident. Other benefits include improved posture, better body shape and skin tone. Exercise helps us deal with anxiety and builds self-esteem: How can we be fit and healthy and not feel good?

"Much satisfaction comes with knowing that you are taking positive steps to allay concerns about health and aging. There is gratification in the sense of control over your own life that results from pursuing a regular exercise program.

"Let's consider how to set up an exercise regime. Knowing that activity brings you more life and gives underexercised bodies a chance to get rid of tension, how does one go about getting the right amount of exercise? For maximum benefit we need to exercise vigorously (exercise-bike, jogging, biking, swimming, rope skipping, running, hiking or brisk walking) three times a week for thirty-minute periods. 'Exercise that requires sustained effort and greater oxygen consumption, and affects the enzyme system by stimulating increased blood flow, muscular exertion, and lung respirations is called aerobic

exercise.[5] A raised pulse rate, maintained over a controlled period of time, is what causes the positive
effects we are seeking, and is called the training
effect. Less exercise than you need or more than the
optimal is not helpful. Our body is designed for action
and movement. Aerobics helps us to keep our organs,
muscles, and brains fit, and counteracts the effects of
aging and arteriosclerosis. Vigorous exercise when combined with a low-fat diet can help you live longer and
live better."

B. Exercise

1. "Think back over the previous twenty-four hours and
   recall when and how you were physically active. Were
   there times during the day when you could have moved
   about more? What could you have done about any of the
   tasks or events of the day to make them more active?
   For example, could you have walked to the store instead of driving your car? Make a list of those
   activities. Also, consider when you can make time
   for physical exercise." Allow about five minutes'
   think time.

2. Ask group members to find partners and share ideas
   for increasing the amount of time spent exercising or
   being more physically active. Allow about five
   minutes.

———————

5. Ardell, High Level Wellness, p. 148.

3. Reassemble the group and ask if anyone would like to share what then learned from the exercise. Was anyone successful in thinking of creative ways to transform a sedentary event or task into an active one? Ask for sharing of plans to build exercise time into daily schedules--especially from people who are not now following an exercise program.

IV. PRACTICE OF DEEP MUSCLE RELAXATION

Read the DMR script from Session 1, pages 22-29. Again, record group members' levels of relaxation achieved on the relaxation scale.

V. HANDOUTS AND HOME ASSIGNMENT

Distribute copies of handouts:

"Benefits of Exercise and Aerobic Exercise Plan," page 114; and "Exercise Dos and Don'ts," page 115.

Remind participants that next week is the last session and that they should be thinking about how they will continue to work on stress management after the workshop ends.

HANDOUTS FOR SESSION 6
IMPROVING MY INTERNAL ENVIRONMENT
WORKSHEET

1. Three persons, places, or things that cause me stress are:

2. One positive or beneficial aspect of each stressor:

3. Something I worry about is:

4. A time I could set aside for a quieting relaxation technique is:

5. Someone I can talk to about worries or problems is:

112

STEPS TOWARD IMPROVING YOUR INTERNAL ENVIRONMENT
Training and Shaping Your Mind

1. Develop a positive attitude toward life
   Stress is useful and necessary
   Seek growth experience
   It's how you take it

2. Learn to take it easy
   We worry too much--use diversion, thought stoppage

3. Set aside quieting time

4. Talk out worries
   Meet with a friend or professional

5. Set your goals to achieve inner peace and serenity
   Accept what you can't change
   Love yourself
   Live fully, enjoy the present

6. Educate your mind
   Read about human growth, stress, etc.
   Arm yourself with knowledge

BENEFITS OF EXERCISE

Regular sessions of physical conditioning--aerobic exercise--
contribute these benefits:

> Increased efficiency of delivery of oxygen to tissues
> Lowered heart rate and blood pressure
> New growth of capillaries to carry more blood to the muscles
> Reduction of body fat
> Increased ability to deal with stress
> Flexibility, endurance, strength
> Resistance to stress, disease, illness
> Better posture, body shape, complexion
> Better tolerance of anxiety
> Self-esteem and feelings of fitness and health

AEROBIC EXERCISE PLAN

Aerobic Exercise

Exercise that requires--

> Sustained effort
> Greater oxygen consumption
> Increased blood flow
> Increased breathing
> Greater muscular exertion

For optimum benefit--
Vigorous exercise three times a week for 30-minute periods

Examples--

| Jogging, running | biking | swimming |
| Hiking | brisk walking | rope skipping |

EXERCISE DOS

Make exercise part of your life; set aside a specific time of day
   for your program.

Select activities you enjoy; have fun when exercising.

Maximize opportunities for activity; replace sedentary habits.

Change your eating habits; overweight is also a serious health
   problem.

Warm up and cool down gradually; three to five minutes before and
   after vigorous exercise.

Be sensible about clothing, shoes, replacing fluid.

Keep up the good work; motivate yourself, exercise with a friend or
   club, read up on your activity.

EXERCISE DON'TS

Don't look at exercise as a "crash" program.

Don't set unrealistic goals.

Don't exercise for at least one to two hours after eating.

Don't continue to exercise if you notice injury or when you're ill
   or suffering from infection.

Don't hurry or rush your program; start gradually, build up your
   time.

Don't forget to check with your doctor before beginning your program,
   especially after age 30.

SESSION 7

BRIEF OUTLINE

OBJECTIVES: To introduce information on diet and nutrition as it
relates to stress management.

To help participants develop personal stress management plans they can carry out after the group experience comes to an end.

To evaluate the group experience and bring the workshop to a suitable closure by finishing any unfinished
business and reviewing with each member his or her
follow-up stress management plans for growth.

I. OPENING THE SESSION--HOME ASSIGNMENT REVIEW

II. STRESS MANAGEMENT PRINCIPLE 5--NUTRITION AWARENESS

III. PERSONAL STRESS MANAGEMENT PLAN

IV. ON-GOING GOALS FOR STRESS MANAGEMENT

V. EVALUATION OF WORKSHOP

SESSION 7

I. OPENING THE SESSION--HOME ASSIGNMENT REVIEW

"This is the last session, an ending but also a beginning, so we shall look at what we accomplished and also plan new beginnings and goals. We shall take time later in the session to begin creating personal stress management plans for ourselves and to share some of our goals for stress reduction after the group ends."

Inquire whether anyone wants to share their efforts to be more physically active. You could begin by giving an example of something you tried during the week.

II. STRESS MANAGEMENT PRINCIPLE 5--NUTRITION AWARENESS

A. Mini-lecture

"Exercise, adequate rest, and stress-reducing approaches such as recreational activities, deep muscle relaxation, meditation, and talking it out will promote health but they are not sufficient for all our needs in handling stress. An important part of any stress management program is a nutritionally sound diet. We need to provide our bodies with the right building and nourishment materials. Attention to proper nutrition is a form of insurance against disease and debilitation. According to Donald B. Ardell, 'A major diet-related health hazard in our country is a combination of over-consumption and under-nutrition.'[1]

"Nutrition research has been conducted and reported by the Human Nutrition Center of the United States Department of Agriculture (USDA), the National Cancer Institute, and the American Heart Association. The Human Nutrition Center has been concerned about the mounting evidence that links many illnesses and premature deaths to our dietary habits.[2] Its experts report that Americans over the past two generations have increased the consumption of fats, refined sugars, and salt. This increase has come about because of

---

1. Donald B. Ardell, <u>High Level Wellness; An Alternative to Doctors, Drugs, and Disease</u> (New York: Bantam, 1977, 1979), p. 113.
2. Sylvia Schur, "Eating Your Way to Health," <u>Parade</u>, July 8, 1978, p. 19.

our high standard of living, our vast and productive
domestic agriculture, and our wealthy status in the world
marketplace. We have a multitude of choices and an abund-
ant supply in the supermarket. We have no difficulty
filling our shopping carts with ever greater quantities of
meat, dairy products, and prepared foods. Without realizing it, we have slowly changed our eating habits over the
years and are now reaping the unhealthful consequences.

"One of the missions of the USDA is to raise our nutritional
consciousness and recommend dietary changes that may reduce
the risk for Americans of heart disease, hypertension,
obesity, diabetes, and some cancers (such as cancer of the
colon and breast cancer), and to increase life expectancy.
We have the option to choose whether or how we might
modify our diet and life-style to improve our health and
perhaps add to our life span.

"First steps toward including diet and nutrition in your
stress plan are to develop nutrition awareness, learn
about new findings based on research, and then map out
your own course. Keep in mind that the subject of diet
and nutrition is a controversial area where different
opinions are held; the final answers are not yet in and
will depend on future research. However, some basic knowledge gives us a useful guide to follow. If you are considering making major dietary changes or if you have a
health problem such as diabetes, ulcers, hypertension,
or cardiovascular disease and plan to change your usual

eating habits, be sure to discuss your plan with your
doctor before beginning.

"There is no miracle pill, food, activity, or relaxation
technique that by itself will be the magic answer to help
us manage stress. Our chances of success are increased
if we take a holistic approach to managing stress by giving
attention to all these areas--physical, mental, and
emotional."

B. Suggested Dietary Changes
    Distribute copies of the handout "Suggested Dietary
    Changes" (see pages 127-28). Briefly go over these
    recommendations with the group, inviting questions or
    reactions. While much of this information about nutrition
    may not be new to participants, they may not have con-
    sidered the role of good nutrition in a stress reduction
    plan.

III. PERSONAL STRESS MANAGEMENT PLAN

Distribute copies of the "Personal Stress Management Plan" (see page 129) to participants. Go over the plan, giving examples of how participants might respond to each section, such as those given in the mini-lecture that follows. Where appropriate, explain how the stress management principles discussed in the workshop can be applied to participant's action plans.

A. <u>Mini-lecture</u>

"This planning process takes a comprehensive approach to assessing and managing stress in your personal life and on the job. Think through your responses carefully in order to formulate a successful plan to manage stress.

"<u>Proper Stress Level</u>:

The kinds of stress you can endure--such as increased responsibilities, if given support.

The kinds of stress you cannot endure--such as isolation; fear of the unknown; lack of information or preparation for a new experience, activity, job.

Your personal rhythmic pattern--What is your best time of day or year? Do you handle beginnings or endings better? Are you a slow starter and fast finisher, or function at a steady, even pace?

"Resources:

 Physical--What is your level of health, energy,
  sleep requirements?

 Emotional--Honestly appraise your emotional
  strengths and weaknesses.

 Social--How well do you relate to others? Do you
  have others you can turn to for support or help
  with problems?

 Intellectual--Give yourself credit for your abilities
  and interests.

 Spiritual--Your beliefs about what really matters.

"Current Stressors:

 What is causing the trouble?--For example, it may be
  family illness or an aging relative who no
  longer can take care of him or herself or
  problems at work.

 Analyze the area of pain--You feel responsible and
  guilty about being unable to provide care for
  an elderly relative, or meet productivity
  expectations at work.

 Where is it coming from?--Yourself and other family
  members, your feelings of responsibility, their
  expectations, work overload?

 Who is involved?--Yourself, the sick elderly relative,
  your critical sister, your demanding boss?

 What are you doing that contributes to the problem?
  --This question is not meant to assign blame,
  but to pinpoint potential areas for intervention. You may have unrealistically high

122

expectations of yourself, expecting that you
should be able to handle additional family
responsibilities and tasks at work without
assistance and then blaming yourself when you
cannot do it all without feeling severely
stressed and endangering your own health.
How could you take care of it yourself?--You could
stop blaming yourself for being human. You
could learn how to assertively ask for help
from your family or boss to find ways to do
what needs to be done. Then, reward yourself
for taking a beginning step to relieve stress.

"Values and Goals, Commitments:
Define goal--To get help with care of sick family
member within two days. To obtain your supervisor's approval to reduce your workload to a
manageable level.
Assess its importance--Top priority
Blocks to goal achievement--Budget limitations restrict your freedom to hire someone to care
for the relative, or additional employees where
you work. Time limitations or systems problems
such as unreasonable contract deadlines can be
major blocks in other situations.
Risks or consequences--Other family members may
refuse your request for help, or consent but
be resentful or angry. On the other hand, a
creative solution may evolve such as a rotating
system of care. Your boss may listen

supportively, but say there is nothing he can
do to help you because the job has got to be
done in so many weeks. Even with a refusal,
you will at least respect yourself for having
been assertive--you will have to decide whether
to remain in such a no-win situation.

Or your boss may respect your willingness to
speak up and risk disapproval and suggest
that a strategy meeting be called with the
department to plan how to present the production
dilemma to the contractor.
Others involved--Neighbors, friends who might help.
Co-workers who may be supportive, offer helpful
ideas, be willing to join you in documenting
the reality and impact of work overload.

"Plan of Action:
Specify specific steps to attain goal--Better time
management might release time to provide some
care. Assertively ask your sister's help; ask
assistance of your next-door neighbor as a
backup or to help once a week. Speak to co-
workers about work overload; assess their
interest in submitting a joint request to the
supervisor to discuss this issue. Assertively
request your supervisor's assistance in planning
your work in order to achieve the goals for your
department without risk to your health.

Assess Progress--Set a date to evaluate your
    success."

B.   <u>Exercise</u>

"Please take about five minutes to answer the following
questions on the management plan. You can complete the
questions later at home.

"Answer only:
    Under 'Current Stressors'--What is causing the trouble?
    Under 'Values and Goals, Commitments'--Define goal,
        specifically what do you want to change?
    Under 'Plan of Action'--Determine specific steps to
        attain goal."

IV. ON-GOING GOALS FOR STRESS MANAGEMENT

"I would like to have each of you share what you have been
thinking about for managing stress after the group ends. Will
each of you take one minute to speak about your goals and
plans for your personal stress management program?"

In this way, solicit positive feedback, suggestions, and comments
from the participants and add anything that you feel would be
helpful for them. This process helps the group members make
the difficult termination by focusing on each person's
individual plan, as opposed to group plans. It adds a sense
of formal closure to the experience.

V. EVALUATION OF WORKSHOP EXPERIENCE

A. Evaluation of Workshop

Distribute copies of "Evaluation of Workshop" (see pages 130-131) for the group members to complete. Stress your need for their honest evaluations and suggestions to help you improve the course and your leadership skills. Emphasize also that this is not a test of their accomplishments in the course, merely a method to evaluate the course.

B. Feelings About Workshop Ending

You can model this activity by sharing your feelings about the workshop ending and then asking for others to volunteer. Five minutes is usually sufficient to allow everyone to express themselves. This period also helps bring the group to emotional closure.

C. Voluntary Sharing of Evaluations

Ask if anyone wants to share any suggestions or comments he or she has about the workshop experience. Some people are not good at expressing themselves in writing; this sharing gives you a good evaluation of how the members feel the workshop was helpful.

D. Graduation Certificates (Optional)

The awarding of certificates provides a visible reward and recognition for the participant, and it is also helpful in maintaining the motivation of the group member to continue growing. See sample on page 132.

HANDOUTS FOR SESSION 7
SUGGESTED DIETARY CHANGES*

1. EAT LESS FAT--Less red meat, more poultry, fish; less butter, lard.

2. REDUCE SATURATED FATS--Highest in top-quality red meats, organ meats, butter, egg yolks, cheeses, lard, hydrogenated fats; use vegetable oil or margarine.

3. SUBSTITUTE SKIM MILK FOR WHOLE MILK

4. REDUCE MEAT INTAKE TO NOT OVER 6-8 oz. PER DAY--Consider other protein sources: tofu, beans, soybeans, corn, barley, oatmeal, whole wheat. Eat more carbohydrates such as rice, noodles, spaghetti, bread, potatoes. This is a shift from the high protein-low carbo-hydrate trend. New findings show a calcium loss with modestly high protein levels.

5. EAT MORE FIBER--Such as whole bran; also whole grains. Increase your intake of fruits and vegetables, eaten raw if possible.

6. REDUCE REFINED SUGARS, FLOURS--Sugar levels are high in soft drinks and desserts, also in many condiments, salad dressings, sauces, breads, crackers. Sugar is needed for energy but it is better to get from complex carbohydrates found in bread and vegetables rather than from the simple sugars such as table sugar, honey and molasses, which raise blood fat and cholesterol levels.

---

* "Nutrition and Your Health, Dietary Guidelines for Americans," USDA and USDHEW Pamphlet, 2/80. Superintendent of Documents, U.S. Government Printing Office, Washington, D.C. 20402.

7. AVOID CARCINOGENS AND
    ADDITIVES--Nitrates are linked with stomach cancer and are
                        found in smoked and cured meats and fish;
                        ham, luncheon meats such as bologna,
                        corned beef, sausage, hot dogs, smoked
                        salmon.

8. EAT LESS SALT--Reduce amounts in cooking. Season with herbs,
                        spices, lemon juice. Keep the salt shaker
                        off the table. Be aware that many
                        processed foods contain salt.

9. DRINK LESS COFFEE
    AND TEA--Caffeine induces acid secretion in the stomach, leading
                        to heartburn and ulcers. Caffeine is now
                        also thought to contribute to heart
                        disease, aterosclerosis and diabetes
                        by increasing free fatty acids in the
                        blood.

10. VITAMINS AND
    MINERALS--A balanced, varied diet should supply most of your
                        needs, but you may want to consider
                        supplementing your diet with Vitamins B,
                        C, and E plus minerals. Check with your
                        doctor regarding your particular needs.

11. REDUCE OR ELIMINATE
    ALCOHOL AND CIGARETTES--Both are known health hazards and
                        contribute to heart disease and circula-
                        tory disease. Heavy cigarette smoking
                        increases the risk of lung cancer and
                        other types of cancer.

128

PERSONAL STRESS MANAGEMENT PLAN

Assess each of the following. In formulating your personal intervention it should prove useful to draw from the five stress management principles reviewed in the workshop.

1. <u>Proper Stress Level</u>: The kinds of stress you can endure
    The kinds of stress you cannot endure
    Your personal rhythmic pattern

2. <u>Resources</u>: Physical
    Emotional
    Social
    Intellectual
    Spiritual

3. <u>Current Stressors</u>: What is causing the trouble?
    Analyze the area of pain
    Where is it coming from?
    Who is involved?
    What are you doing that contributes to the
        problem?
    How could you take care of it yourself?

4. <u>Values and goals, commitments</u>: Define goal--specifically what
        do you want to change and
        when?
    Assess importance of the goal
    Blocks to goal achievement
    Risks and/or consequences to
        each action
    Others involved

5. <u>Plan of Action</u>: Determine specific steps to attain goal
    Assess progress
    Alternatives (if indicated)

EVALUATION OF WORKSHOP

We would like to know if this program was helpful to you. Please give your honest opinion and ask the leader if there is any question that you do not understand.

Please circle the number that best indicates your opinion.

	Not at all			Very much	
Do you feel that coming to the meetings helped you?	1	2	3	4	5
How much encouragement and understanding did you feel from other group members?	1	2	3	4	5
Did the group help you feel better about yourself?	1	2	3	4	5
Did the leader - understand your concerns?	1	2	3	4	5
enjoy leading the group?	1	2	3	4	5
plan with the group for the meetings?	1	2	3	4	5
know the subject matter being discussed?	1	2	3	4	5

The most important three things I got out of the group meetings were - - -

Do you handle _____ differently since coming to the group?

Yes _____   No _____

If yes, can you tell what has changed?

Did your attitudes change regarding _____

Yes _____   No _____

If yes, can you tell how your attitudes have changed?

If you were to improve the group, what would you do?

I would like to learn more about . . .

Did you make new friends in the group?   None   few   some   many

Would you recommend this group to your friends?

Yes _____   No _____

Why?

Family Service Association
of Greater Boston
hereby Certifies that

_____

has successfully completed a course
sponsored by the Family Life Education Department on

_____

Awarded at Boston Massachusetts, this
day of _____ nineteen hundred and _____

_____   _____
Director of the Family Life Education Program

BIBLIOGRAPHY

Ardell, Donald B. High Level Wellness: An Alternative to Doctors, Drugs, and Disease. New York: Bantam Books, 1977, 1979.

Benson, Herbert. The Relaxation Response. New York: Morrow, 1975.

Carrington, Patricia. Freedom in Meditation. New York: Anchor Books, 1978.

Davidson, Richard J. and Schwartz, Gary E. "Matching Relaxation Therapies to Types of Anxiety: A Patterning Approach," in Relax: How You Can Feel Better and Reduce Stress and Overcome Tension. Edited by John White and James Fadiman. New York: The Confucian Press, 1976.

Davidson, Jim. Effective Time Management. New York: Human Sciences Press, 1978.

Friedman, Meyer and Rosenman, Ray H. Type A Behavior and Your Heart. New York: Fawcett Crest Books, 1974.

Holmes, Thomas H. and Rahe, Richard H. "The Social Readjustment Rating Scale." Journal of Psychosomatic Research 11 (1967): 213-18.

Jacobson, Edmund. Progressive Relaxation. Chicago: University of Chicago Press, 1929.

Jaffe, Dennis T. Healing From Within. New York: Knopf, 1980.

McLean, Alan A. Work Stress. New York: Addison-Wesley, 1979.

"Nutrition and Your Health, Dietary Guidelines for Americans." USDA and USDHEW pamphlet 2/80. Write to Superintendent of Documents, U.S. Government Printing Office, Washington, D.C. 20402.

Pelletier, Kenneth. Mind as Healer, Mind as Slayer. New York: Delacorte, 1977.

Selye, Hans. The Stress of Life. Rev. ed. New York: McGraw-Hill, 1978.

Simon, Sid. _Meeting Yourself Halfway_. Niles, Ill.; Argus
     Communications, 1974.

Warshaw, Leon J. _Managing Stress_. New York: Addison-Wesley, 1979.

Wolpe, Joseph and Lazarus, Arnold A. _Behavior Techniques: A Guide
     to the Treatment of Neuroses_. Oxford, England: Pergamon
     Press, 1966.